EMOTIONAL INTELLIGENCE DECODED

IMPROVE RELATIONSHIPS, SOCIAL SKILLS AND RESILIENCE. MASTER EMPATHY, SELF AWARENESS AND CONTROL YOUR EMOTIONS. GET SUCCESS IN YOUR PERSONAL LIFE AND THE WORKPLACE.

FREEDOM PUBLICATIONS

Copyright © 2025 Freedom Publications. All rights reserved.

The content within this book may not be reproduced, duplicated, or transmitted without direct written permission from the author or the publisher.

Under no circumstances will any blame or legal responsibility be held against the publisher, or author, for any damages, reparation, or monetary loss due to the information contained within this book, either directly or indirectly.

Legal Notice:

This book is copyright protected. It is only for personal use. You cannot amend, distribute, sell, use, quote, or paraphrase any part of the content within this book, without the consent of the author or publisher.

Disclaimer Notice:

Please note the information contained within this document is for educational and entertainment purposes only. All effort has been expended to present accurate, up-to-date, reliable, and complete information. No warranties of any kind are declared or implied. Readers acknowledge that the author is not engaged in the rendering of legal, financial, medical, or professional advice. The content within this book has been derived from various sources. Please consult a licensed professional before attempting any techniques outlined in this book.

By reading this document, the reader agrees that under no circumstances is the author responsible for any losses, direct or indirect, that are incurred as a result of the use of the information contained within this document, including, but not limited to, errors, omissions, or inaccuracies.

TABLE OF CONTENTS

Introduction   5

1. FOUNDATIONS OF EMOTIONAL INTELLIGENCE   9
   1.1 Scientific Roots and Research   11
   1.2 Emotional Intelligence vs. IQ   14
   1.3 The Emotional Brain: How It Works   16
   1.4 The Five Pillars of Emotional Intelligence   18

2. SELF-AWARENESS AS THE KEY TO GROWTH   21
   2.1 Self-Reflection Practices for Growth   23
   2.2 The Role of Mindfulness in Self-Awareness   25
   2.3 Emotional Agility: Navigating Personal Challenges   27
   2.4 Tools for Self-Assessment and Reflection   29

3. MASTERING SELF-REGULATION   33
   3.1 Managing Emotional Hijacking   35
   3.2 Stress Management through Mindfulness   37
   3.3 Building Resilience in Adversity   39
   3.4 The Art of Patience in Emotional Control   41

4. EMPATHY IN ACTION   45
   4.1 Active Listening: A Pathway to Understanding   47
   4.2 Bridging the Empathy Gap   49
   4.3 Role-Playing to Foster Empathetic Skills   51
   4.4 Empathy in Digital Communication   53

5. EFFECTIVE COMMUNICATION SKILLS   57
   5.1 Overcoming Communication Barriers   59
   5.2 The Power of Vulnerability in Dialogue   61
   5.3 Conflict Resolution with Emotional Intelligence   63
   5.4 Enhancing Social Radar for Better Interactions   65

6. BUILDING AND SUSTAINING RELATIONSHIPS   71
   6.1 The Dynamics of Trust and Empathy   73
   6.2 Relationship Building in Multicultural Settings   75

    6.3 Emotional Intelligence in Parenting   77
    6.4 Emotional Agility in Family Dynamics   79

7. EMOTIONAL INTELLIGENCE IN LEADERSHIP   83
    7.1 Building Emotionally Intelligent Teams   85
    7.2 Conflict Resolution in Leadership   87
    7.3 Motivating and Inspiring Others   89
    7.4 Navigating Change with Emotional Intelligence   91

8. EMOTIONAL INTELLIGENCE FOR PERSONAL GROWTH   95
    8.1 Overcoming the Inner Critic   98
    8.2 Emotional Intelligence and Personal Fulfillment   100
    8.3 Emotional Intelligence and Mental Health   102
    8.4 Harnessing Emotional Strengths for Success   104

9. OVERCOMING BARRIERS AND OBJECTIONS   107
    9.1 Time Management for Personal Development   109
    9.2 Personalized Strategies for Emotional Growth   111
    9.3 Overcoming Skepticism with Practical Results   116

10. APPLYING EMOTIONAL INTELLIGENCE IN REAL LIFE   119
    10.1 Navigating Major Life Transitions   122
    10.2 Cultivating a Culture of Emotional Intelligence   124

    Conclusion   131
    References   135
    About the Publisher   139

INTRODUCTION

There was a pivotal moment in my career when I realized the true power of emotional intelligence. As I stood in front of my team, trying to navigate a complex project that had everyone on edge, I could see the tension and frustration etched on their faces. That's when it hit me, success isn't just about technical skills or IQ, it's also about understanding and managing our emotions and those of the people around us.

This realization sparked a journey of self-discovery and a deep dive into the world of emotional intelligence. Through my research and personal experiences, I've come to understand that emotional intelligence is the key to unlocking our full potential in both our personal and professional lives.

In today's fast-paced, ever-changing world, emotional intelligence has never been more crucial. Studies have shown that *individuals with high emotional intelligence are more likely to succeed in their careers, enjoy healthier relationships, and lead more fulfilling lives.* In fact, a recent study by TalentSmart found that 90% of top performers have high emotional intelligence.

But what exactly is emotional intelligence, and how can we cultivate it? That's what this book, "Emotional Intelligence Decoded," aims to explore. Throughout these pages, we'll delve into the core components of emotional intelligence, including self-awareness, empathy, effective communication and resilience.

As someone who has experienced firsthand the transformative power of emotional intelligence, I'm passionate about sharing this knowledge with others. I've seen how developing my own emotional intelligence has helped me build stronger relationships, communicate more effectively, and navigate challenges with greater ease.

In this book, we'll take a step-by-step approach to understanding and enhancing your emotional intelligence. Each chapter will focus on a specific aspect of emotional intelligence, providing you with actionable strategies, real-world examples, and practical insights that you can apply in your daily life.

We'll start by exploring the foundations of emotional intelligence, including how to recognize and manage your own emotions. From there, we'll move on to building empathy and understanding other people's perspectives, a critical skill for fostering strong relationships. We'll also tackle effective communication strategies, learning how to express ourselves clearly and listen actively to others.

As we progress through the book, we'll examine how emotional intelligence can help us build resilience in the face of adversity and how to use our emotions as a source of strength and motivation. We'll also explore the role of emotional intelligence in leadership and how it can help us inspire and guide others towards success.

By the end of this book, you'll have a comprehensive understanding of emotional intelligence, plus a toolkit of strategies to help you apply it in your own life. You'll be equipped to build stronger, more meaningful relationships, communicate more effectively, and navigate life's challenges with greater resilience and adaptability.

So, are you ready to unlock the power of emotional intelligence and transform your life? Then let's dive in together and discover the heart of human connection. With an open mind and a willingness to learn, you'll be amazed at the incredible potential that lies within you.

CHAPTER 1
FOUNDATIONS OF EMOTIONAL INTELLIGENCE

Have you ever found yourself in a meeting, nodding along as if you understood everything, but inside, you were wrestling with a whirlwind of emotions? Maybe your colleague just snagged the project you were hoping to get, and you're trying to mask that twinge of envy with a smile. Welcome to the vibrant, sometimes chaotic world of emotional intelligence. It's a world where understanding your feelings and those of others, can be your secret weapon for personal and professional triumphs. *Emotional intelligence, also known as EQ,* (Emotional Quotient), isn't just about being nice or agreeable, it's about perceiving, assessing, and managing emotions, both yours and those around you. It's a skill set, not unlike learning to ride a bike, and once you get the hang of it, it can change how you navigate life's bumpy roads.

It's worth pointing out that even though Emotional Intelligence (EI) and Emotional Quotient (EQ) are often used interchangeably, they are different:

- **Emotional Intelligence (EI)** refers to the ability to **recognize, understand, manage, and influence emotions,** both in yourself and in others. It is a broad concept that includes skills like self-awareness, empathy, emotional regulation, and social skills.
- **Emotional Quotient (EQ)** is a **measurement** of Emotional Intelligence, similar to how IQ (Intelligence Quotient) measures cognitive intelligence. EQ is often assessed through tests and scales to determine how well a person applies emotional intelligence in real-life situations.

So, while people often use **EQ** and **Emotional Intelligence** interchangeably, technically, **EI is the ability**, and **EQ is the score or measurement** of that ability.

In our modern society, where interactions are more digital than ever, emotional intelligence is crucial. Texts, emails, and those endless Zoom meetings can often strip away the nuances of face-to-face communication, leaving us guessing at the emotions behind the words. A study from TalentSmart found that 90% of top performers possess high emotional intelligence, underscoring its impact on career success. From fostering better personal relationships to excelling professionally, understanding EQ can be your guiding star. It's not just about getting along; it's about thriving, about turning your interactions into meaningful connections and your challenges into opportunities for growth.

Emotional intelligence first made waves in the academic world in 1990, thanks to psychologists Peter Salovey and John D. Mayer. They laid the groundwork by defining emotional intelligence as a set of skills that allow us to accurately appraise, express and regulate emotions. Fast forward a few years and Daniel Goleman popularized the concept with his groundbreaking book, making emotional intelligence a household term. Goleman's work expanded on Salovey and Mayer's ideas, illustrating how emotional intelligence affects everything from relationships to workplace dynamics.

Now, before we dive in, let's make ourselves familiar with some more key terms that will pop up throughout our journey. First, there's EQ or Emotional Quotient, which, as noted above, is a measure of your emotional intelligence, much like IQ measures cognitive abilities. Then there's **empathy**, the ability to truly understand and share the feelings of others. It's like putting on someone else's shoes and walking a mile in them, without actually getting blisters. **Self-regulation** is another biggie. It's about keeping your emotions in check, so you don't end up sending that angry email you'll regret later. Finally, **social skills** encompass everything from communication to conflict resolution, making them the glue that holds our interactions together.

Exercise: How Emotionally Intelligent Are You?

Take a moment to reflect on a recent interaction that left you feeling either proud or a little regretful. Jot down what emotions you experienced and how you reacted. Were you aware of your feelings at the time, or did they surprise you later? Consider how you might respond differently next time, using your newfound understanding of emotional intelligence. This simple exercise can be your first step towards heightened self-awareness, setting the stage for the deeper insights you'll gain as you explore the pages ahead.

1.1 SCIENTIFIC ROOTS AND RESEARCH

Let's take a moment to step behind the curtain and explore the fascinating science that supports emotional intelligence. You might think of your brain as a busy airport, with emotions acting like planes ready for takeoff. The control tower here is the limbic system, the grand orchestrator of emotions, behaviors, and memories. This network of brain structures, including the amygdala and the hippocampus, acts as the seat of our emotional intelligence. The amygdala, for instance, is like a fire alarm, reacting instantaneously to threats with a swift emotional response. On the other hand, the prefrontal cortex, located just behind your forehead, acts as the wise old sage, helping regulate these emotional outbursts by applying logic and reason. The interaction between these regions is crucial for emotional intelligence, as it allows us to not only feel but also process and control those feelings.

Our understanding of emotional intelligence has been shaped by a host of psychological theories and research methodologies. Studies have delved into how cognitive processes influence emotional regulation and vice versa. For example, researchers have used functional MRI scans to observe brain activity, revealing how different areas light up in response to emotional stimuli. These studies have shown that emotional intelligence is not just about feelings, but involves an intricate connection between *emotions and cognition*. This scientific exploration helps explain why someone with high emotional intelligence can navigate complex social landscapes with grace, making it not just a desirable trait but a vital skill in today's world.

Significant research findings have also highlighted the *correlation between emotional intelligence and leadership effectiveness*. Studies have consistently shown that leaders with high emotional intelligence are more effective at guiding their teams and inspiring others. They have the uncanny ability to tune into the emotional undercurrents of a group, fostering an environment where people feel understood and valued. Emotional intelligence is also a predictor of mental health outcomes, with higher levels often linked to better psychological well-being. People with strong emotional intelligence skills tend to experience *less anxiety and depression*, as they possess the tools to manage their emotions and build supportive relationships.

Of course, like any field, emotional intelligence has its critics. Some argue that measuring emotional intelligence is challenging due to its subjective nature. Unlike IQ, which can be quantified with standardized tests, EQ is more nuanced, relying on self-assessments and peer evaluations. There's also an ongoing debate about whether emotional intelligence should be considered a distinct form of intelligence or if it overlaps significantly with personality traits. Despite these debates, the practical applications of emotional intelligence research continue to expand.

In educational settings, emotional intelligence is being integrated into curricula to help students develop social and emotional skills alongside academic knowledge. It's not just about learning math or history anymore; it's about understanding oneself and others, which can lead to a more holistic education. In the corporate world, emotional intelligence training programs have become commonplace, helping employees improve teamwork, communication, and leadership skills. Businesses have recognized that fostering emotional intelligence can lead to better productivity and a more harmonious workplace.

Case Study: Emotional Intelligence in Action

Consider a multinational corporation that decided to implement emotional intelligence workshops across its global offices. The aim was to improve team dynamics and enhance leadership skills. Within a year, the company reported a noticeable increase in employee engagement and a decrease in staff turnover. Managers noted that teams were more collaborative and communicative, tackling projects with a newfound sense of camaraderie and understanding. This case study underscores the tangible benefits of prioritizing emotional intelligence, not just as a concept, but as a practical tool for success in any field.

1.2 EMOTIONAL INTELLIGENCE VS. IQ

Imagine sitting in a dimly lit room, trying to piece together a complex puzzle. Some pieces represent logic and reasoning, while others reflect emotions and relationships. This puzzle is a metaphor for the interplay between Intelligence Quotient (IQ) and Emotional Intelligence Quotient (EQ). IQ measures cognitive abilities, think logic, math, and memory. It's the part of your brain that aces standardized tests and solves Sudoku puzzles in record time. In contrast, EQ is the social and emotional compass, guiding you through the nuances of human interactions. EQ involves understanding and managing your emotions, empathizing with others, and navigating social complexities. Together, they create a fuller picture of human potential.

In the realm of success, IQ and EQ serve distinct purposes. Imagine a brilliant scientist who can solve complex equations but struggles to collaborate with colleagues. Here, IQ shines in academic and technical fields, where cognitive prowess is paramount. However, in leadership and interpersonal relationships, EQ takes the spotlight. Picture a manager who inspires their team with empathy and understanding, fostering an environment where everyone thrives. EQ enables leaders to connect with others, resolve conflicts, and motivate teams. While IQ might get you in the door, EQ ensures you thrive once inside, building bridges and fostering collaboration.

Balancing IQ and EQ is like walking a tightrope, where both elements are crucial for maintaining equilibrium. Consider well-known figures who have excelled with both high IQ and EQ. Think of renowned entrepreneurs who have innovated groundbreaking technologies while leading diverse teams with empathy and vision. These individuals understand that success in the fast-paced world demands both cognitive skills and emotional acumen. For instance, when faced with a high-stakes negotiation, EQ helps read the room and manage emotions, while IQ analyzes data and strategizes solutions. The combination allows for informed, empathetic decision-making.

Now, let's address some common misconceptions that often lead to confusion. One myth suggests that EQ is more vital than IQ or vice versa. In reality, they complement each other like peanut butter and jelly; each brings something unique to the table. EQ isn't about being overly emotional, nor is IQ about being cold and detached. Instead, they work together, enhancing each other's strengths. Imagine a team where analytical thinkers collaborate with emotionally intelligent leaders, creating a dynamic environment where ideas flourish and challenges are met with creativity and empathy.

Emotional intelligence, while sometimes overshadowed by the traditional emphasis on IQ, plays a significant role in shaping success. Imagine a workplace where emotional intelligence is prioritized alongside cognitive skills. Here, employees aren't just problem solvers; they're communicators, team players, and empathetic leaders. They understand not only the intricacies of their work but also the emotions and motivations of their colleagues. This balanced approach creates a more holistic, productive, and harmonious environment.

In conclusion, the synergy between IQ and EQ is crucial for navigating the complexities of life. Neither should be underestimated or overvalued. Instead, they should be seen as complementary forces that, when combined, create a powerful tool for personal and professional success. Acknowledging the importance of both allows individuals to leverage their strengths, address their weaknesses, and cultivate a more balanced approach to success.

1.3 THE EMOTIONAL BRAIN: HOW IT WORKS

Picture your brain as a bustling metropolis, each area a neighborhood buzzing with activity, each pathway a busy street connecting ideas, feelings, and actions. At the heart of this city lies the limbic system, the emotional headquarters, tirelessly regulating and processing emotions. It's like the city's emotional pulse, ensuring that everything from joy to fear gets its due attention. The limbic system is home to the amygdala, a small yet powerful neighborhood known for its swift emotional responses. Ever found yourself reacting impulsively when your buttons are pushed? That's the amygdala springing into action, sometimes a bit too enthusiastically, prompting those knee-jerk reactions we often wish we could take back.

The prefrontal cortex, located just behind your forehead, acts as the wise elder of the brain city, reigning in the amygdala's impulsivity with reasoned thought and judgment. This area is crucial for self-control and decision-making, enabling you to pause and think before acting. Imagine a scenario where you receive an email that instantly riles you up. Instead of firing off a fiery response, your prefrontal cortex steps in, urging you to take a deep breath and draft a more measured reply. It's this balancing act between the amygdala and prefrontal cortex that forms the cornerstone of emotional regulation, allowing you to navigate complex emotional landscapes with finesse.

Neuroplasticity, the brain's impressive ability to reorganize itself, plays a starring role in enhancing emotional intelligence. Think of it as your brain's potential for a makeover, reshaping itself through practice and experience. Research shows that by engaging in brain training exercises, such as mindfulness and empathy practices, you can strengthen neural pathways, making emotional regulation more intuitive. Just as lifting weights builds muscle, consistent practice in emotional awareness can enhance your brain's emotional capabilities, ultimately improving your emotional intelligence.

The link between *emotional intelligence and mental health* is both profound and encouraging. Studies have found that individuals with higher emotional intelligence experience lower levels of anxiety and depression. This is because emotional intelligence equips you with the tools to better understand and manage your emotions, reducing the likelihood of being overwhelmed by them. Consider techniques like journaling, where you reflect on daily emotions and their triggers, or mindfulness meditation, which promotes emotional awareness and resilience. These practices empower you to approach emotions with curiosity and compassion, improving overall psychological well-being.

Imagine a world where everyone takes a few moments each day to nurture their emotional intelligence. It's a world where understanding emotions becomes as natural as breathing, and where mental health flourishes alongside emotional awareness. In this world, people communicate openly, conflicts are resolved with empathy, and relationships are built on a foundation of mutual understanding. Emotional intelligence becomes not just a skill but a way of life, enriching every interaction and experience.

1.4 THE FIVE PILLARS OF EMOTIONAL INTELLIGENCE

Imagine emotional intelligence as a sturdy five-legged stool, each leg representing a critical pillar that supports your ability to navigate life's ups and downs with finesse. First up is *self-awareness*, the ability to recognize and understand your own emotions. It's like having a personal weather forecast for your moods, helping you anticipate emotional storms before they hit. Consider those days when stress looms large, and you're about to snap at the barista for getting your order wrong. Recognizing that a stress trigger is self-awareness in action, allowing you to take a deep breath and find calm before reacting.

Next, we have *self-regulation*, the art of keeping your emotions in check, even when you're boiling inside. Picture a heated argument where your anger threatens to take over, making you say things you'll regret later. Self-regulation steps in like a wise friend whispering, "Take a moment, breathe, and think before you speak." It's the difference between escalating a conflict and resolving it peacefully. This pillar gives you the grace under pressure that can turn potential disasters into opportunities for understanding and growth.

Motivation is the third pillar, and it's the spark that propels you toward your goals. It's not just about ambition; it's about finding that inner drive when the going gets tough. Think of motivation as the engine that fuels your pursuit of personal and professional achievements. Whether it's setting a goal to run a marathon or launching a new project at work, motivation keeps you going. It transforms setbacks into stepping stones and challenges into chances to prove your mettle.

Empathy, the fourth pillar, is like slipping on someone else's shoes to understand their journey. It's about seeing the world through another's eyes and feeling their emotions as your own. In a workplace setting, empathy means appreciating your colleague's perspective during a heated discussion. Instead of dismissing their concerns, you listen actively and acknowledge their feelings, creating a collaborative and supportive environment. Empathy is the glue that binds teams together, fostering trust and mutual respect.

Finally, we have *social skills*, which are the tools you use to build relationships and navigate social interactions. Whether it's networking at a conference or building rapport with a new neighbor, social skills play a vital role in your everyday life. They enable you to communicate effectively, resolve conflicts, and create meaningful connections. Think of social skills as the bridge that connects your inner world with the outer one, allowing you to thrive in diverse settings and situations.

These five pillars don't stand alone; they interact and support each other, creating a dynamic framework for emotional intelligence. Self-awareness enhances empathy by helping you understand your own emotions, making it easier to relate to others. Motivation fuels your social skills, encouraging you to reach out and connect with people, even when you're feeling shy or uncertain. Together, these pillars form a balanced approach to emotional intelligence, allowing you to navigate life's complexities with confidence and poise.

Developing all five pillars is crucial. Focusing on just one can leave you lopsided, much like a stool missing a leg. A balanced approach ensures you're prepared for any emotional scenario that life throws your way. Strategies for growth include practicing mindfulness to boost self-awareness, setting personal goals to enhance motivation, and engaging in active listening exercises to develop empathy. The benefits of cultivating emotional intelligence are numerous, from improved relationships and increased resilience to greater career success and personal fulfillment.

In the end, emotional intelligence is not just about understanding and managing emotions; it's about living a richer, more connected life. By nurturing these five pillars, you equip yourself with the tools to build stronger relationships, overcome challenges, and achieve your goals. It's a lifelong process of growth and learning, where each step forward brings you closer to becoming the best version of yourself.

CHAPTER 2
SELF-AWARENESS AS THE KEY TO GROWTH

Imagine you are cruising down the highway of life, windows down, music blasting, when suddenly, a red light of emotion flares up out of nowhere. You slam on the brakes, wondering what just happened. Welcome to the realm of emotional triggers. These are the invisible potholes on your emotional journey, those sudden jolts that make you react in ways you didn't expect. *Emotional triggers* are deeply rooted responses that influence your behavior, thoughts, and feelings. They're like those sneaky speed bumps you never see coming, yet they can send your emotions into a tailspin, impacting everything from your mood to your relationships.

Let's unpack the mystery of emotional triggers. Imagine a colleague offers some "constructive criticism" on your latest project. Suddenly, you feel your face heating up, your heart racing faster than a kid on a sugar rush. That's your body's physiological response to a trigger, courtesy of the limbic system and its trusty sidekick, the amygdala. This brain region processes emotions like fear and anxiety, and when triggered, it can flood your system with stress hormones such as cortisol, making your body react as if it's under attack. Common triggers can range from criticism, rejection, and even those moments when you feel invisible or dismissed. The impact? Anything from a mild annoyance to a full-blown emotional roller coaster ride.

Recognizing your personal triggers is like being a detective in your own emotional mystery. Start by keeping a *trigger journal*. Note down those moments when your emotions skyrocket, like when your boss assigns that last-minute project or your partner forgets your anniversary. Writing helps capture the context and your emotional reaction, illuminating patterns you might otherwise miss. Another approach is *situational analysis*. Reflect on daily interactions and pinpoint what sets you off. Is it a particular tone of voice? A specific phrase? By identifying these triggers, you can begin to take control and prevent them from derailing your day.

Understanding the origins of these triggers often requires a trip down memory lane. Childhood experiences can leave lasting imprints, shaping how you respond to similar situations as an adult. Maybe you were often told to "toughen up" or "stop crying," leading you to feel vulnerable when criticized. Cultural and societal influences also play a significant role. Society might value stoicism, encouraging you to hide emotions rather than express them. These influences combine to form your unique emotional landscape, impacting how you react to the world around you.

Now, let's talk solutions. When a trigger hits, breathing exercises can be your first line of defense. Simple *deep-breathing techniques* can help reduce stress and ground you in the moment, like a mental reset button. Cognitive reframing is another powerful tool. This involves shifting your perspective on the triggering situation. Instead of viewing criticism as a personal attack, try seeing it as an opportunity for growth and improvement. This mental shift can help reduce the emotional charge associated with the trigger and open doors to constructive dialogue.

Exercise: Identifying Your Triggers

Grab a notebook and dedicate a page to tracking your emotional triggers. For a week, jot down moments when you notice a strong emotional reaction. Note the situation, your immediate feelings, and any physical responses. Reflect on these entries at the end of the week. What patterns do you see? Are there recurring themes or specific scenarios that trigger you? Use this insight to develop strategies to manage your responses proactively.

By understanding and managing your emotional triggers, you take a vital step toward enhanced self-awareness and emotional intelligence. You become the driver of your own emotional vehicle, equipped to handle whatever curves or bumps the road may throw your way.

2.1 SELF-REFLECTION PRACTICES FOR GROWTH

Let's talk about *self-reflection*, that trusty friend who never judges, always listens, and occasionally nudges you toward those "aha" moments. It's like holding a mirror up to your soul, allowing you to see the inner workings of your mind and heart. Self-reflection is more than just thinking about your day; it's the cornerstone of emotional growth and self-awareness. Through introspection, you can better understand your personal values and beliefs, those beliefs that influence your decisions and reactions. It's about asking yourself the hard questions: What truly matters to me? Why do I react the way I do? This practice helps clarify what drives you, what holds you back, and what empowers you to move forward. When you reflect regularly, you hold yourself accountable, ensuring that your actions align with your values. It's a tool for personal and emotional accountability, a means to track your growth and development over time.

Journaling is one of the most effective self-reflection tools, and it's accessible to everyone. Think of it as your private space to explore thoughts and emotions without any filters. Start by setting aside a few minutes each day to write down your emotions and reactions to the day's events. You might be surprised at what surfaces when you put pen to paper. Consider using daily prompts to guide your writing, questions like "What emotion did I feel most strongly today?" or "Was there a moment that surprised me?". These prompts help you zero in on specific emotional experiences, making it easier to identify patterns over time. As you review your journal entries, look for recurring themes or triggers that emerge. Do certain situations consistently evoke strong emotions? Recognizing these patterns is the first step toward understanding and managing your emotional landscape.

Meditation is another powerful practice for self-reflection, offering a moment of quiet in the chaos of everyday life. Mindfulness meditation, in particular, encourages you to observe your thoughts without judgment, like clouds passing through the sky. It's about being present, noticing the ebb and flow of your mind, and letting go of distractions. This practice enhances self-awareness by helping you become more attuned to your thoughts and emotions. Another technique is body scan meditation, where you focus on physical sensations, moving through each part of your body with gentle attention. This practice connects you to both your body and mind, allowing you to explore how emotions manifest physically. Over time, meditation fosters a deeper understanding of yourself, promoting resilience and emotional balance.

Evaluating personal growth is crucial, yet it often slips through the cracks in our busy lives. Start by setting clear, achievable growth goals. Maybe you want to respond more calmly under pressure or improve your ability to empathize with others. Write these goals down, and revisit them regularly to track your progress. Reflect on the steps you've taken and celebrate even small victories along the way. Another valuable tool is feedback from trusted friends or mentors. They can offer perspectives you might not see yourself, shedding light on areas where you've grown or where you might need a little more work. Embrace this feedback with an open heart, using it as a guide to refine your path toward personal growth.

2.2 THE ROLE OF MINDFULNESS IN SELF-AWARENESS

Picture yourself in a bustling coffee shop, the aroma of freshly brewed beans swirling around you, yet your mind is miles away, tangled in thoughts about tomorrow's presentation or last night's awkward dinner conversation. This is where mindfulness can work its magic. Mindfulness is about being present in the moment, tuning in to your current experiences without letting your mind wander off into the depths of past regrets or future worries. It's akin to pressing pause on the chaos and simply being. The benefits are substantial, improved focus, better emotional regulation, and a noticeable reduction in stress. Imagine being able to filter out the noise and zero in on what truly matters, whether it's savoring that first sip of coffee or engaging more deeply in a conversation with a friend. It's about finding clarity amidst the clutter, allowing you to respond to life's challenges with a calm mind and an open heart.

To integrate mindfulness into everyday life, start with simple exercises that don't require hours of meditation or a trip to a secluded mountaintop. Begin with mindful breathing, a grounding practice where you focus on each breath as it flows in and out. Find a quiet spot, close your eyes, and take a few deep breaths, paying attention to the sensation of the air entering and leaving your body. It's a mini-vacation for your mind, a chance to step back and reset. Then there's walking meditation, which turns a simple stroll into a mindful journey. As you walk, notice the rhythm of your steps, the feeling of the ground beneath your feet, and the sights and sounds around you. This practice invites you to engage with your surroundings fully, transforming an ordinary walk into an extraordinary moment of awareness.

The impact of mindfulness on brain function is nothing short of fascinating. Regular mindfulness practice has been shown to bring about changes in brain structure, particularly in areas related to self-awareness and emotional regulation. Studies reveal that mindfulness can lead to a thicker prefrontal cortex, the part of the brain responsible for complex behaviors and decision-making. It also affects the amygdala, the emotional center of the brain, helping to reduce its activity and, in turn, lowering stress levels. It's like giving your brain a workout, strengthening the pathways that promote calmness, clarity, and resilience. This doesn't just happen overnight; it's a gradual process, much like building muscle through regular exercise. But with time, these changes can lead to a more balanced and focused mind, better equipped to handle the ebbs and flows of daily life.

Mindfulness and emotional intelligence go hand in hand. Mindfulness enhances your ability to empathize with others, as it encourages you to be present and truly engage with the emotions of those around you. When you practice mindfulness, you cultivate a greater understanding of your own emotions, which in turn helps you relate to others with more compassion and insight. It's like tuning into the emotional frequency of those you interact with, making connections more meaningful and authentic. Additionally, mindfulness plays a crucial role in improving emotional regulation. When you're mindful, you're better able to recognize your emotions as they arise, giving you the space to choose how to respond rather than reacting impulsively. This leads to more thoughtful interactions and harmonious relationships, both personally and professionally.

2.3 EMOTIONAL AGILITY: NAVIGATING PERSONAL CHALLENGES

If you were a surfer, balancing on your board as a wave barrels toward you, *emotional agility* is your ability to ride that wave without wiping out. It's about navigating your emotions with skill and ease, adapting to whatever life throws your way. Emotional agility isn't just about feeling good; it's about understanding your emotions, recognizing their value, and responding to them with intention. This skill is crucial for personal growth, allowing you to adapt to change, manage stress, and overcome obstacles. When you cultivate emotional agility, you become more flexible in your thinking and behavior, opening the door to new possibilities and solutions.

Developing emotional agility requires practice and intention. One technique is to accept your emotions without judgment. This means acknowledging your feelings, whether they're joyful or uncomfortable, without labeling them as good or bad. By accepting your emotions, you create space for reflection and understanding. Another strategy is to use your core values as a compass for decision-making. When faced with a difficult choice or a challenging situation, ask yourself what truly matters to you.

Aligning your actions with your values helps you stay true to yourself, even in the face of adversity.

Emotional agility and resilience go hand in hand. Resilience is your ability to bounce back from setbacks, and emotional agility provides the tools to do just that. Consider someone who loses their job unexpectedly. Instead of being overwhelmed by fear and uncertainty, an emotionally agile person acknowledges their emotions and uses them to fuel their next steps. They might reflect on their values and decide to pursue a new career path that aligns more closely with their passions. By staying open to change and adapting their approach, they demonstrate resilience and strength.

Real-world examples of emotional agility are all around us. In the workplace, conflicts are inevitable. Picture a team member who disagrees with a decision made during a meeting. Instead of reacting defensively, they take a moment to understand their emotions and the underlying reasons for their discomfort. They then engage in a constructive conversation, expressing their concerns respectfully and collaboratively seeking a solution. This approach not only resolves the conflict but also strengthens team dynamics and fosters a culture of open communication.

Personal stories often illustrate the power of emotional agility. Imagine someone navigating a significant life transition, such as moving to a new city. Initially, they might feel overwhelmed by the change and unsure of how to adapt. Yet, by embracing their emotions and using them as a guide, they gradually find their footing. They explore their new surroundings, connect with others, and discover opportunities they hadn't imagined. Through this process, they grow more confident and resilient, demonstrating the transformative potential of emotional agility.

Emotional agility is a dynamic skill that empowers you to face life's challenges with confidence and grace. By developing this ability, you can navigate personal and professional setbacks more effectively, turning obstacles into opportunities for growth and learning. Whether you're handling workplace conflicts, making difficult decisions, or navigating life changes, emotional agility equips you with the tools to move forward with resilience and purpose. It's a skill that enriches your relationships, enhances your well-being, and opens the door to a more fulfilling and adaptable life.

2.4 TOOLS FOR SELF-ASSESSMENT AND REFLECTION

Sometimes managing your emotions can feel like trying to navigate a foreign city without a map or self-assessment. *Self-assessment* acts as that trusty map, helping you pinpoint where you are and where you need to go. It's about recognizing your strengths and weaknesses, giving you a clearer picture of your emotional landscape. By understanding what makes you tick and where you might stumble, you can better prepare for life's emotional twists and turns. Self-assessment isn't just about identifying flaws; it's about celebrating your strengths and using them to bolster areas that need attention. It's like looking in a mirror that reflects not just your face, but your inner workings, allowing you to approach each day with a sense of clarity and purpose.

Thanks to the digital age, self-assessment tools are just a click away. Online emotional intelligence quizzes provide a quick snapshot of your current emotional skills. They're like a friendly nudge, highlighting areas that might need a bit more TLC. Additionally, self-assessment inventories are more comprehensive, offering a deeper dive into your emotional competencies. These tools often come with tailored feedback, guiding you on how to enhance your emotional strengths and address any weaknesses.

While these tools are not a magic bullet, they are a great starting point for anyone looking to better understand their emotional blueprint.

Feedback from others is an invaluable aspect of self-assessment. It's like having a trusted advisor who sees things you might miss. Constructive feedback from peers, colleagues, or mentors can open your eyes to blind spots and highlight areas for growth. It can be difficult to hear sometimes, but remember, it's an opportunity to learn and improve. In professional settings, 360-degree feedback offers a holistic view, providing insights from various angles, whether it's your boss, your team, or even your clients. By gathering feedback from a diverse group, you gain a well-rounded understanding of your emotional impact on others and can make more informed decisions about your personal development.

Creating a personal development plan is your blueprint for turning insights into action. Start by setting specific, achievable goals for enhancing your emotional intelligence. Maybe you want to improve your active listening skills, respond more calmly to stress, or cultivate greater empathy in your relationships. Write these goals down, and outline the steps needed to achieve them. Consider using techniques like SMART goals, making them Specific, Measurable, Achievable, Relevant, and Time-bound, to keep you on track. Regularly review your plan, tweaking it as needed, much like a gardener tending to their plants. Track your progress through journals, feedback, and self-assessment tools, celebrating milestones along the way. It's a dynamic process, requiring patience and persistence, but the rewards will be a more self-aware, emotionally intelligent you, and are well worth the effort.

As you gain clarity and understanding, remember that self-assessment is a lifelong process. It's not about achieving perfection but about continuous growth and learning. Whether through online tools, feedback from others, or a structured development plan, you hold the keys to unlocking deeper self-awareness and emotional intelligence. As you move forward, these practices will guide you in building a solid foundation for personal growth, paving the way for more meaningful connections and a greater sense of fulfillment in your life.

CHAPTER 3
MASTERING SELF-REGULATION

If you're on a tightrope, balancing above a sea of swirling emotions, trying not to topple into the abyss of an emotional outburst, *self-regulation* is your balancing pole, offering stability as you navigate life's inevitable emotional storms. Picture a time when you felt ready to explode, whether from stress, anger, or frustration, and consider how mastery of self-regulation could have transformed that moment into one of calm and control. Emotional regulation is the key to this balance, a skill that empowers you to manage your emotions proactively rather than reactively, turning potential chaos into clarity.

At the heart of emotional regulation lies cognitive restructuring, a technique that helps you change negative thinking patterns into more balanced and realistic thoughts. Think of it as a mental renovation, where you identify faulty thought patterns and rebuild them into a healthier framework. Say goodbye to black-and-white thinking or catastrophizing, and welcome a more nuanced perspective. By questioning assumptions and gathering evidence, you can challenge automatic negative thoughts (ANTs) and replace them with productive alternatives. This transformation not only reduces stress and anxiety but also improves communication and relationships, as you approach situations with a clearer, more grounded mindset.

Another powerful tool in your emotional toolbox is *emotion labeling*, a strategy that involves identifying and naming your emotions. It's like giving your feelings a name tag at a party, allowing you to acknowledge and understand them without letting them hijack your mind. By labeling your emotions, you gain control over them, as you can address their root causes rather than being swept away by them. It's about pausing to say, "Ah, that's frustration I'm feeling," and then deciding how to address it constructively. Recognizing emotions and their triggers is the first step to selecting appropriate regulatory strategies, empowering you to navigate emotional challenges with confidence.

The process of emotional regulation begins with identifying the emotion you're experiencing and its trigger. Imagine a situation where you're feeling overwhelmed at work. Is it an impending deadline, a difficult colleague, or something else entirely? By pinpointing the trigger, you gain insight into why you're feeling the way you do. Once identified, the next step is selecting an appropriate regulatory strategy. This could involve cognitive restructuring, emotion labeling, or other techniques tailored to your specific needs. The goal is to find a strategy that helps you manage your emotions effectively, preventing them from spiraling out of control and affecting your mental health or relationships.

Emotion regulation plays a crucial role in maintaining mental health and interpersonal relationships. By managing your emotions, you reduce anxiety and prevent stress from escalating into more serious issues. This regulation also enhances your relationship dynamics, as you're better equipped to communicate and empathize with others. When you regulate your emotions, you're less likely to react impulsively, leading to more thoughtful and respectful interactions. It's about creating a positive cycle of emotional awareness and control that benefits both you and those around you.

Exercise: Journaling for Emotional Processing

Grab a notebook or open a digital document and set aside a few minutes each day for journaling. Focus on processing your emotions by writing about a specific situation that triggered a strong emotional response. Describe the emotion, its trigger, and how you reacted. Reflect on how you might use cognitive restructuring or emotion labeling to approach similar situations in the future. This exercise not only enhances your emotional awareness but also provides valuable insights into your emotional patterns, helping you develop more effective regulatory strategies.

Role-playing scenarios can also be a practical exercise for honing your emotional regulation skills. Gather a friend or colleague and create scenarios that might trigger strong emotions, such as a tense conversation or a challenging decision. Practice responding to these scenarios using the techniques discussed, such as cognitive restructuring or emotion labeling. By rehearsing these responses, you build confidence in your ability to handle similar situations in real life, turning potential emotional pitfalls into opportunities for growth and understanding.

3.1 MANAGING EMOTIONAL HIJACKING

Imagine you're at a family dinner, and someone brings up politics, the very topic you vowed to avoid. Suddenly, you feel a surge of heat rising from your chest to your cheeks, and before you know it, you're embroiled in a heated argument you didn't plan to have. Welcome to the world of *emotional hijacking*, where your rational brain takes a backseat and your emotions grab the steering wheel. Coined by Daniel Goleman, emotional hijacking describes those moments when the amygdala, the emotional epicenter of your brain, overrides your logical thinking. It's as if someone hit the fast-forward button on your emotions, leaving you in the aftermath to pick up the pieces. In high-stress situations, these hijacks can lead to decisions that feel good in the moment but may not serve you in the long run. Whether it's snapping at a loved one or sending an impulsive email you'll later regret, emotional hijacking can derail your day and strain your relationships.

Recognizing when you're in the throes of an emotional hijack is the first step toward regaining control. Picture yourself in a tense meeting, and suddenly, you feel your heart pounding like a drum, your face gets flushed, and you notice your voice rising. These physical sensations often accompany emotional hijacks and serve as red flags. Another tell-tale sign is a sudden urge to make a rash decision, like quitting your job on a whim or storming out of a room. It's that overwhelming feeling that your emotions are calling the shots, while your rational self seems to have taken a coffee break. Understanding these signs can help you pause and take a step back before you act, allowing you to reclaim the steering wheel from your emotions.

So, how do you prevent emotional hijacking from taking over? One of the quickest ways to calm the emotional storm is through breathing exercises. The next time you feel an emotional hijack coming on, try the 4-7-8 breathing technique. Inhale through your nose for a count of four, hold your breath for seven seconds, and exhale through your mouth for eight seconds. This simple exercise can help slow your heart rate, giving you a moment to collect your thoughts and decide how best to proceed. Grounding techniques are another effective strategy. When emotions threaten to sweep you away, focus on the sensations around you. Feel your feet on the ground, notice the texture of the chair you're sitting on, or listen for the ambient sounds in the room. These *grounding techniques* can anchor you in the present, providing a buffer between you and your emotional impulses.

Building long-term resilience against emotional hijacking involves cultivating emotional stability over time. One of the most effective ways to do this is by developing a strong emotional support network. Think of your support network as a safety net that catches you when you're on the brink of an emotional hijack. Surround yourself with people who understand you, offer perspective, and can help you process your emotions constructively. Whether it's a trusted friend, a family member, or a professional counselor, having someone to turn to can make all the difference. Regular mindfulness practice is another powerful tool for enhancing emotional resilience. By incorporating mindfulness into your daily routine, you train your brain to stay present, reducing the likelihood of being swept away by emotional hijacks. Mindfulness encourages you to observe your thoughts and emotions without judgment, allowing you to respond to situations with clarity and intention. Over time, these practices can help you build a robust defense against the emotional hijacks that life inevitably throws your way.

3.2 STRESS MANAGEMENT THROUGH MINDFULNESS

Imagine your mind as a bustling city during rush hour, thoughts zipping around like cars, emotions honking for attention, and stress weaving through it all like a persistent traffic jam. This is where mindfulness comes in, like an expertly timed stoplight that brings order to the chaos. *Mindfulness* is a powerful tool for managing stress, helping to reduce the physiological responses that often accompany it. When practiced regularly, mindfulness can act like a calming balm, soothing frayed nerves and bringing your system back into balance. It's not about eliminating stress entirely, that would be like trying to stop the tide, but rather it's like learning to ride the waves with poise and clarity.

Mindfulness techniques specifically geared toward stress reduction can be game-changers. Take body scan meditation, for example. This practice invites you to focus on the physical sensations in your body, moving from head to toe like a gentle mental massage. It's about tuning into the subtle sensations, tension in your shoulders, the rise and fall of your chest, and acknowledging them without judgment. This awareness can help you release physical stress, leaving you feeling more grounded and centered. Another technique is guided imagery, where you visualize calming scenes, maybe a serene beach or a tranquil forest. Letting your mind wander to these peaceful places can promote deep relaxation and alleviate stress.

Incorporating mindfulness into your daily routine can transform your overall well-being. It's like adding a touch of clarity, calm, and coolness to your everyday hustle. Regular mindfulness practice can lead to improved concentration and focus, allowing you to tackle tasks with greater efficiency and clarity. It also enhances emotional control, helping you navigate tricky situations with a cool head rather than a hot temper. The anxiety levels that once felt like a constant companion can begin to subside, replaced by a sense of calm and control. Think of mindfulness as your mental fitness routine, building resilience and reducing stress one breath at a time.

The concept of mindful pauses can be a lifesaver when stress threatens to overwhelm. It's about taking a brief timeout to reset and recharge, like hitting the refresh button on your mental browser. Imagine you're in the middle of a hectic workday, and stress is beginning to creep in. Pause for a moment, close your eyes, and take a few deep breaths. Allow yourself to become aware of your surroundings, the sensation of your chair, the sounds in the room, and the feeling of your breath. These mindful pauses can prevent stress from escalating, anchoring you in the present moment, and providing a space for reflection and clarity.

Implementing mindful breaks during work can be as simple as setting a timer to remind you to pause throughout the day. Use this time to engage your senses, notice the texture of your desk, listen to the subtle hum of the office, or take a moment to enjoy the scent of your coffee. These *sensory awareness practices* can anchor you in the present, helping to stave off stress and maintain a sense of equilibrium. Think of them as micro-vacations for your mind, keeping you refreshed and ready to tackle whatever comes your way.

3.3 BUILDING RESILIENCE IN ADVERSITY

Life has a funny way of throwing curveballs, doesn't it? Just when you think you've got everything under control, something unexpected happens, a job loss, a breakup, or even a global pandemic, and suddenly, you're in the deep end without a floatie. This is where resilience comes into play, acting as your lifeline. Resilience is your ability to bounce back from setbacks, to dust yourself off and keep moving forward, no matter how hard you've been knocked down. It's not about never falling; it's about getting back up each time you do. In the grand scheme of emotional regulation, resilience is what keeps you steady when the ground beneath you feels shaky.

Resilient individuals often share a few key traits that help them to weather life's storms with a little more ease. For starters, they tend to have a growth-oriented mindset, seeing challenges as opportunities rather than insurmountable obstacles. They're the ones who can look at a glass that's half-empty and see it as full of possibilities. Optimism, however, doesn't mean they're constantly wearing rose-colored glasses; it's more about finding the silver lining in tough situations. Alongside this mindset, they possess strong problem-solving skills, enabling them to navigate through difficulties with creativity and perseverance. They can look at a tangled mess and find a way to unravel it, one knot at a time. These traits make them adaptable, allowing them to adjust their sails when the winds of life change direction.

So, how can you build resilience in the face of adversity? One effective method is developing adaptive coping mechanisms. This involves learning to manage stress in healthy ways, whether through exercise, hobbies, or simply a good old-fashioned venting session with a friend. Another approach is fostering a supportive social environment. Surround yourself with people who lift you up, who remind you of your strengths when you've forgotten them. A strong network can offer perspective and encouragement, helping you see the light at the end of the tunnel, even when it feels dim. Additionally, it's about cultivating an environment where you feel safe to take risks and make mistakes, knowing you have a safety net to catch you if you fall.

Real-world examples of resilience are both inspiring and instructive. Take, for instance, a young entrepreneur who, after experiencing a series of business failures, finally hits their stride with a startup that takes off. Instead of seeing those initial failures as the end, they viewed them as stepping stones, learning from each mistake and applying those lessons to their next venture. Or consider an individual who, after enduring the loss of a loved one, finds solace and healing by volunteering, channeling their grief into helping others. These stories highlight the power of resilience in turning life's challenges into catalysts for growth and transformation.

In professional settings, resilience can manifest in various ways. Imagine a team facing a significant project setback, like a product launch delay. Rather than throwing in the towel, resilient team members come together to brainstorm solutions, tackling each obstacle with determination and creativity. By fostering a culture of resilience, organizations can navigate challenges more effectively, emerging stronger and more cohesive. These examples illustrate that while life can be unpredictable and sometimes downright tough, resilience allows you to face adversity head-on, emerging wiser and more grounded.

3.4 THE ART OF PATIENCE IN EMOTIONAL CONTROL

Picture yourself waiting in line at the grocery store, and the person in front of you is taking forever to count their coupons. Your foot starts tapping, your mind races, and *impatience* bubbles to the surface. We've all been there, caught in the grip of impatience when life refuses to follow our timetable. Patience, however, is more than just waiting without grumbling; it's a vital component of emotional control that acts as a buffer against impulsive reactions. It's like a sturdy dam holding back the floodwaters of hasty decisions and emotional outbursts. Patience allows you to pause, reflect, and choose your response with care, rather than letting emotions dictate your actions.

Developing patience requires practice, much like building muscle at the gym. Start with mindful breathing exercises. When you feel impatience creeping in, take a slow breath in, hold it for a moment, and then release it gently. This simple act can slow down your racing thoughts and bring you back to the present moment. Practicing delayed gratification is another method. Challenge yourself to resist immediate rewards in everyday scenarios, like waiting a few extra minutes before indulging in your favorite snack. This practice strengthens your patience muscle, making it easier to handle life's bigger frustrations with composure.

Patience and emotional intelligence are best friends, each enhancing the other. Patience fosters empathy, especially through patient listening. When you take the time to truly listen without interrupting, you open yourself to understanding others' perspectives. This not only enriches your connections but also deepens your emotional insight. Likewise, patience leads to improved decision-making. By taking a moment to consider your options thoughtfully, you make decisions that are more aligned with your values and less driven by fleeting emotions. It's about giving yourself the gift of time to process information, consider consequences, and act with intention.

To cultivate patience in real life, you can engage in timed activities that practice waiting without distraction. Set a timer and dedicate a short period to simply sitting in a quiet space, resisting the urge to check your phone or fidget. This exercise sharpens your ability to sit with discomfort and reinforces your patience. Reflective writing on experiences that test your patience can also be enlightening. Jot down moments when impatience flared and how you responded. Consider what you might do differently next time. This reflection can reveal patterns and offer insights into how patience can be further nurtured.

Patience is more than a virtue. It's a crucial skill that enhances emotional control and intelligence. By weaving patience into the fabric of your daily life, you create space for empathy, thoughtful consideration, and meaningful connections. Remember that patience isn't about waiting passively but waiting actively, with awareness and intention. It's the quiet strength that allows you to navigate the ups and downs of life with grace and wisdom. As you cultivate patience, you'll find that those long lines, delayed plans, and unexpected detours become opportunities, not obstacles in your journey of emotional growth.

By embracing the practices and perspectives of emotional regulation, hijack prevention, stress management, resilience building, and patience cultivation, you're equipping yourself with a comprehensive toolkit for mastering self-regulation. These skills will not only enhance your personal growth but also enrich your relationships and professional endeavors. As you continue to explore the depths of emotional intelligence, you'll discover the profound impact of self-regulation on your journey. In the next chapter, we will delve into the transformative power of empathy, exploring how deeply understanding others can elevate your emotional intelligence and strengthen your connections with those around you.

CHAPTER 4
EMPATHY IN ACTION

So, you're at a party, chatting away, when suddenly the host's cat bolts across the room, sending a tray of hors d'oeuvres flying. As chaos ensues, you notice your friend's face crumple in embarrassment, their efforts to keep the party perfect unraveling in an instant. In that moment, you feel their distress as if it's your own, and you quickly step in to help clean up, offering a reassuring smile. This is empathy at work, our ability to understand and share the feelings of others, bridging the gap between our own experiences and theirs. It's a powerful tool that can transform our relationships, allowing us to connect on a deeper level and foster meaningful connections.

Before we dive deeper, let's untangle the *difference between empathy and sympathy. Sympathy* is like standing on the sidelines and feeling sorry for someone, while *empathy* is jumping into the trenches with them, feeling their emotions from their perspective. According to 'Verywell Mind', empathy means understanding a person from their frame of reference rather than your own. It's a cornerstone of relationship building, offering a pathway to deeper connections that sympathy alone can't provide. Where sympathy might lead to judgment, empathy promotes a non-judgmental understanding by truly exploring another person's thoughts and feelings.

Now, how can you cultivate this essential skill? One effective strategy is *perspective-taking*, which involves putting yourself in someone else's shoes and seeing the world through their eyes. Imagine you're driving to work and someone cuts you off. Instead of honking in frustration, consider that they might be rushing to an emergency. This shift in perspective can help diffuse anger and foster understanding. *Emotional mirroring* is another technique, where you reflect the emotions of others to connect with their feelings genuinely. If a friend is sharing their struggles, acknowledging their pain by saying, "That sounds really tough," can validate their emotions and strengthen your bond.

Of course, empathy doesn't come without its challenges. Biases and stereotypes often cloud our ability to empathize, creating barriers that prevent us from fully connecting with others. Recognizing these biases is the first step toward overcoming them. It requires a conscious effort to question our assumptions and open our minds to different perspectives. Reducing emotional burnout is also crucial for maintaining empathy. Constantly absorbing others' emotions can be draining, leading to empathy fatigue. To combat this, prioritize self-care and set boundaries to recharge your emotional reserves.

The transformative power of empathy extends beyond personal relationships, impacting professional dynamics as well. Empathy can turn workplace conflicts into opportunities for collaboration and growth. Take the case of a team struggling with communication issues. By fostering an environment of empathy, team members learn to listen actively and appreciate each other's viewpoints, leading to improved collaboration and harmony. In the realm of conflict resolution, empathy serves as a powerful tool. When parties in a disagreement take the time to understand each other's emotions, they lay the groundwork for finding common ground and reaching a resolution.

Empathy Reflection Exercise

Set aside a few moments each day to practice empathy. Reflect on a recent interaction where you felt disconnected from someone. Consider their perspective and emotions. What might they have been feeling, and how could you have shown empathy in that situation? Jot down your thoughts and revisit them regularly to track your progress in developing a more empathetic mindset.

Empathy isn't just a skill; it's a gateway to richer, more fulfilling relationships. By embracing empathy, you open yourself to a world of understanding and connection, where differences become opportunities for growth rather than barriers. As you continue to practice empathy, you'll find that it enriches every interaction, bringing you closer to the people around you and fostering a sense of belonging and compassion.

4.1 ACTIVE LISTENING: A PATHWAY TO UNDERSTANDING

Imagine sitting across from someone who's talking, but all you hear is the distant hum of their words. That's hearing, just the passive act of sound waves hitting your eardrums. Active listening, on the other hand, is like tuning into a radio station with perfect clarity. It's about engaging fully with what's being said, not just nodding along while crafting your next clever retort in your head. Active listening enhances empathetic connections by allowing you to truly understand the speaker's emotions and thoughts. It's a pillar of effective communication, transforming interactions from surface-level chats into meaningful exchanges. Active listening requires you to be present, to suspend your own judgments and biases, and to genuinely absorb what the other person is expressing. By doing so, you cultivate a deeper understanding that fosters trust and intimacy, whether it's with a coworker sharing a project update or a friend confiding in you about their latest life dilemma.

Becoming an attentive listener is an art form that anyone can master with a bit of practice. Start with the basics, maintain eye contact, which signals to the speaker that they have your full attention. Complement this with nonverbal cues like nodding or leaning slightly forward, which show you're engaged and interested. Next, try paraphrasing and summarizing what the speaker says. This technique not only demonstrates that you're truly listening but also clarifies any misunderstandings. For instance, you might say, "So what I'm hearing is that you're feeling overwhelmed at work, right?" This invites the speaker to confirm or correct your interpretation, ensuring that both parties are on the same page. Finally, sprinkle in some open-ended questions to encourage the speaker to elaborate. Instead of asking, "Are you okay?" you might try, "Can you tell me more about what's been going on?" This approach opens the door for deeper dialogue, allowing the speaker to explore their thoughts and feelings in a safe, supportive environment.

Of course, active listening isn't without its hurdles. In our fast-paced, tech-driven world, staying focused can be a challenge. Distractions abound, from the ping of an incoming email to the buzz of a notification. To manage these interruptions, try setting aside dedicated time for conversations, ensuring that both you and the speaker can engage without competing distractions. Another common pitfall is letting assumptions cloud your understanding.

It's easy to jump to conclusions based on past experiences or preconceived notions, but doing so can derail genuine communication. Combat this by practicing mindfulness, which encourages you to stay present and approach conversations with curiosity rather than judgment.

The benefits of active listening extend across various settings, enriching both professional and personal interactions. In the workplace, active listening can significantly enhance teamwork. Imagine a project meeting where every team member feels heard and understood. This fosters a collaborative spirit, where ideas flow freely and creative solutions emerge. In personal settings, active listening can strengthen family bonds. Picture a family dinner where everyone puts down their devices and listens attentively to one another. This creates an atmosphere of respect and appreciation, where each person's thoughts and feelings are valued.

Active listening transforms mundane interactions into opportunities for connection and growth. By cultivating this skill, you enhance your relationships, build trust, and create a foundation for meaningful communication that resonates with others and enriches your life.

4.2 BRIDGING THE EMPATHY GAP

If you were standing on one side of a canyon, trying to communicate with someone on the other side, would your communication be 100% successful? You can see them, shout across, maybe even wave, but something's missing: a connection. This canyon represents the empathy gap, a void that can arise from cultural differences, technology, or even our own biases. It's the distance that keeps us from fully understanding and empathizing with others. Cultural differences, for instance, can act like a thick fog, obscuring our ability to see the world from another's perspective. What might be a sign of respect in one culture can be perceived as indifference in another. Navigating these differences requires not only knowledge but also an openness to learn and grow beyond our comfort zones.

Technology, too, plays its part in widening this gap. While it connects us across continents, it can also create a sense of detachment. Screens filter out the nuances of face-to-face interaction, leaving us with emojis that struggle to convey the depth of human emotion. The absence of physical presence can lead to misunderstandings, making it more challenging to relate to others. In a world where virtual interactions are increasingly common, finding ways to infuse empathy into digital communication is crucial. It requires a conscious effort to read between the lines and to humanize our interactions, remembering there's a person with emotions on the other side of that screen.

So, how do we start building bridges across this gap? Engaging in cross-cultural dialogues is one powerful approach. By actively seeking out conversations with people from different backgrounds, you open the door to understanding diverse experiences. It's like adding new colors to your palette, enriching your worldview with every exchange. Practicing empathy in virtual environments is another key strategy. When interacting online, be mindful of tone and intent, and strive to put yourself in the other person's shoes. Acknowledge that the absence of physical cues requires extra effort to communicate with clarity and compassion, turning technology from a barrier into a tool for connection.

Vulnerability plays a pivotal role in closing the empathy gap. By sharing your personal stories, you invite others into your world, fostering trust and understanding. It's like opening the curtains to let the sunlight in, revealing the common threads that bind us as humans. Encouraging vulnerability in safe, supportive spaces allows for deeper connections, where people feel seen and heard. When you share your struggles and triumphs, you create a ripple effect, inspiring others to do the same. This openness not only bridges gaps but also strengthens the fabric of your relationships, weaving together experiences that transcend cultural or technological divides.

Real-world examples abound of empathy successfully closing gaps. Community projects that bring diverse groups together can foster empathy and collaboration. Imagine a neighborhood initiative where residents from different backgrounds come together to create a community garden. As they work side by side, they share stories, learn from each other, and build a sense of belonging. In the corporate world, initiatives that promote inclusive and empathetic cultures can transform workplaces. Companies that prioritize empathy training and encourage open dialogues create environments where employees feel valued and understood. These efforts lead to stronger teams and more innovative solutions, as diverse perspectives come together to shape a shared vision.

4.3 ROLE-PLAYING TO FOSTER EMPATHETIC SKILLS

Imagine stepping into someone else's shoes, not just metaphorically, but literally acting out their experiences, emotions, and reactions. That's the essence of role-playing, a method as effective in classrooms and boardrooms as it is in the theater. It's that magical school where empathy isn't just taught but experienced firsthand. Role-playing allows you to dive deep into emotions and perspectives you might never encounter otherwise, expanding your emotional repertoire and enhancing your empathetic abilities. In educational and professional settings, role-playing serves as a dynamic tool for empathy development, turning abstract concepts into tangible experiences. By participating in role-playing exercises, you engage your mind and emotions, discovering new facets of empathy and understanding along the way.

But how do you ensure that role-playing is more than just a fun activity? Start by creating scenarios grounded in real-life situations. The more authentic the scenario, the more impactful the exercise. Whether it's a workplace conflict or a social dilemma, the key is to make it relatable. This authenticity encourages participants to fully immerse themselves in their roles, exploring emotions and reactions with honesty and openness. After the role-play, take time to debrief. This reflection phase is crucial, as it allows participants to discuss what they felt, learned, and how they might apply these insights in real-life interactions. It's about connecting the dots between the role-play and everyday life, cementing the lessons learned in the process.

Engaging in role-playing exercises can have a profound impact on empathy improvement. As you slip into various roles, your emotional intelligence and perspective-taking skills naturally increase. You start noticing nuances in emotions, understanding motivations, and recognizing the complexity of human interactions. This enhanced empathy can lead to better management of interpersonal conflicts, as you become adept at seeing situations from multiple viewpoints. Imagine a workplace where team-building exercises incorporate role reversals. Employees might switch roles with colleagues, gaining insight into each other's challenges and responsibilities. This newfound awareness fosters empathy, leading to more harmonious and efficient team dynamics.

Role-playing has found its place in numerous successful applications, from workshops to team-building activities.

Consider workshops designed to teach conflict resolution through role-playing. Participants might act out a disagreement between coworkers, exploring different approaches to resolving the conflict. By experiencing the situation from various angles, they develop a better understanding of the factors at play and discover effective strategies for resolution. Similarly, team-building exercises can promote empathy and collaboration. Picture a team where members take turns playing the role of a frustrated customer, while others practice empathetic listening and problem-solving. Through these exercises, empathy becomes a shared language, enabling teams to work together more effectively and compassionately.

Role-playing isn't just a tool; it's a transformative experience that fosters empathy and understanding. By stepping into others' shoes, you expand your emotional horizons, enhancing your ability to connect with and support those around you. Whether in a classroom, workplace, or community setting, role-playing offers a unique and powerful way to cultivate empathy, creating a ripple effect of compassion and connection.

4.4 EMPATHY IN DIGITAL COMMUNICATION

Imagine having a heartfelt conversation where you can only use text. Emojis and GIFs become your makeshift facial expressions, and the challenge is to convey warmth and understanding through a screen. Welcome to the digital age, where empathy faces new challenges. Gone are the comforting cues of a nod or a reassuring smile. The absence of these nonverbal signals can make digital interactions feel cold and impersonal. Without the subtle hints of tone, pitch, and body language, it's easy to misinterpret intentions or miss the emotional depth behind words. The internet's anonymity can also strip away the human touch, reducing complex feelings to binary exchanges. People may say things online that they would never dream of uttering face-to-face, leading to misunderstandings and a lack of empathetic engagement.

But all is not lost in the digital realm. There are ways to foster empathy in online communication, starting with the language we choose. Emotive language, sprinkled with well-placed emojis, can add layers of warmth and nuance to our messages. A simple "How are you?" can morph into a genuine inquiry with the addition of a smiling or concerned emoji. Mindful communication is another key strategy, akin to pausing before hitting send. Take a moment to consider the clarity and context of your message. Are you leaving room for misinterpretation? If you're sharing feedback or discussing a sensitive topic, ensure that your words reflect empathy and understanding. This approach can help reduce miscommunications that often arise in the digital space, where tone is easily lost in translation.

In virtual teams, empathy plays a pivotal role in maintaining effective collaboration. Building rapport and trust isn't just about sharing a physical office space. It's about creating an environment where team members feel valued and understood, even from miles away. Encourage open communication and feedback, where everyone has a voice and feels comfortable expressing their thoughts and concerns. This openness fosters a culture of trust, where empathy thrives and collaboration flourishes. Regular check-ins, virtual coffee breaks, or team-building activities can nurture these connections, making remote work more engaging and cohesive.

Examples of digital empathy in action abound. Consider a virtual team that prioritizes empathy in its interactions. They might start meetings with personal check-ins, inviting members to share how they're feeling that day. This simple practice builds camaraderie, reminding everyone that they're not just colleagues but human beings navigating the same uncertain waters. On social media, campaigns that promote empathetic interactions create ripples of positivity. For instance, initiatives encouraging people to share stories of kindness or support can transform digital platforms into spaces of connection and understanding, where empathy is the currency that binds us together.

Empathy in digital communication isn't just a nice-to-have; it's a necessity in our interconnected world. By embracing strategies that enhance empathy online, we can bridge the gaps created by screens and distance, fostering connections that are as meaningful as those shared in person. As we continue to explore the depths of empathy in our interactions, let's remember that our digital words carry the power to heal, support, and unite across the vast expanse of cyberspace.

As we conclude this exploration of empathy, consider how these insights can transform your digital interactions. In the next chapter, we'll delve into communication skills that further enhance your emotional intelligence, building on the empathetic foundation we've established.

CHAPTER 5
EFFECTIVE COMMUNICATION SKILLS

One day, you're having a chat with a friend, and suddenly, words spill out like a waterfall. But instead of clarity, there's a flood of confusion. Welcome to the challenge of expressing feelings, a task that can sometimes feel as daunting as herding cats. This is where emotional literacy steps in, acting as your trusty guide through the labyrinth of emotions. Emotional literacy is the ability to recognize, understand, and articulate your emotions effectively. It's not just about knowing that you're angry, but understanding why and being able to communicate it clearly without turning into a human volcano. Think of it as equipping yourself with a robust emotional toolkit, enhancing your ability to connect with others and manage your mental health. According to Study.com, emotional literacy builds on emotional intelligence, allowing for more effective communication and healthier relationships.

Emotional literacy empowers you to navigate social interactions with finesse, enhancing both personal and professional relationships. Imagine it as a flashlight, illuminating the path to understanding and clarity. By mastering emotional literacy, you can articulate your feelings with precision, reducing misunderstandings and building trust. It's about transforming those vague, swirling emotions into clear, actionable expressions. This skill is a cornerstone of personal empowerment, allowing you to take charge of your emotional world. Just as a painter uses a palette of colors to create a masterpiece, emotional literacy enables you to use a rich vocabulary to express the full spectrum of your feelings.

One effective strategy for boosting your emotional expression is using "I" statements. These statements help you take ownership of your emotions, ensuring that you communicate your feelings without placing blame. Instead of saying, "You make me so angry," you might try, "I feel frustrated when..." This shift from accusatory language to personal expression fosters understanding and reduces defensiveness. Another technique is expanding your emotional vocabulary. Just as a chef needs a variety of ingredients to create a delicious dish, a rich emotional vocabulary allows you to articulate your feelings more accurately. Practice using specific words to describe your emotions, moving beyond generic terms like "sad" or "happy" to more nuanced expressions like "disappointed" or "elated."

The impact of emotional literacy on relationships is profound. When you express your emotions clearly, you pave the way for transparent communication, building trust and mutual respect. It's like opening a window to your inner world, inviting others to understand and appreciate your perspective. This openness reduces the likelihood of misunderstandings, as you articulate your feelings with clarity and confidence. In professional settings, emotional literacy enhances teamwork and collaboration. By expressing your emotions effectively, you contribute to a positive work environment where colleagues feel valued and heard.

Emotional Literacy Exercise

Set aside a few minutes each day for journaling. Focus on identifying and naming your emotions as you reflect on your experiences. Try to capture the nuances of your feelings, using specific words to describe them. For example, instead of writing, "I felt bad," you might say, "I felt disappointed and slightly anxious." This exercise helps you enhance your emotional articulation skills, allowing you to express your feelings with greater clarity.

Role-playing scenarios can also be a valuable tool for practicing emotional expression. Gather a friend or colleague and create scenarios that require you to express complex emotions, such as discussing a misunderstanding or navigating a difficult conversation. Practice articulating your feelings using "I" statements and your expanded emotional vocabulary. This exercise builds your confidence in expressing emotions, preparing you for real-life interactions.

By developing emotional literacy, you equip yourself with the skills to navigate the intricacies of human emotions with grace and confidence. It's about transforming your emotional landscape into a tapestry of understanding and connection, enriching your relationships and enhancing your communication skills.

5.1 OVERCOMING COMMUNICATION BARRIERS

Imagine being at a bustling international conference, surrounded by people speaking a mix of languages, each bringing their own cultural nuances. You're trying to connect with a colleague from a different part of the world, but their expressions and gestures seem foreign, almost like trying to decipher an ancient manuscript. This is where communication barriers rear their head, causing misunderstandings and confusion. *Language* and *cultural differences* often top the list of obstacles, making it challenging to convey intentions and emotions accurately. What might be a simple nod of understanding in one culture could be perceived differently in another, like a game of charades gone awry. Emotional barriers, such as fear or anxiety, can also hinder effective communication. They act like invisible walls, keeping us from expressing ourselves openly or interpreting others' messages clearly. Ever felt your heart race during a heated discussion, words tangled up in your throat? That's anxiety playing its part, making it harder to say what you mean and mean what you say.

Luckily, there are strategies to navigate these barriers, turning potential communication roadblocks into bridges of understanding. Active listening and empathy are your trusty companions when bridging cultural gaps. By truly listening, you open yourself to understanding different perspectives, allowing you to connect on a deeper level. It's like switching from mono to stereo, enriching the conversation with layers of meaning. When faced with language differences, patience and empathy become crucial. Take a moment to acknowledge the other person's efforts to communicate, offering gentle encouragement rather than impatience. Use clear, simple language and visual aids if needed, helping to paint a clearer picture of your message. Managing emotional reactions during conversations is another essential skill. When anxiety or fear creeps in, take a deep breath and focus on your intention to connect rather than the emotion itself. Techniques like pausing to collect your thoughts or using open-ended questions can defuse tension, transforming potential misunderstandings into opportunities for clarity.

Emotional intelligence plays a starring role in overcoming communication barriers, acting like a well-tuned compass guiding you through the complexities of human interaction. By using empathy, you can step into someone else's shoes, understanding their experiences and emotions. It's like getting a backstage pass to their world, enriching your connection with insights and compassion. Emotional regulation helps prevent defensive reactions, allowing you to respond thoughtfully rather than impulsively. Picture a conversation where someone critiques your work. Instead of reacting defensively, emotional intelligence helps you pause, consider their perspective, and respond constructively. This approach not only preserves the relationship but also fosters a culture of open dialogue and collaboration.

Consider a *multicultural* team meeting where members hail from diverse backgrounds. Initially, misunderstandings abound, with cultural nuances lost in translation. But by embracing active listening and empathy, team members learn to appreciate each other's perspectives, bridging gaps with patience and understanding. Visual aids become invaluable, providing a universal language that transcends words. Over time, this approach transforms potential conflict into a rich tapestry of collaboration, where differences are celebrated rather than feared. On a more personal note, imagine someone overcoming a language barrier through sheer determination and empathy. By patiently learning a few key phrases in their colleagues' language and embracing cultural differences, they build rapport and trust, turning a once-daunting obstacle into a shared experience of growth and connection.

5.2 THE POWER OF VULNERABILITY IN DIALOGUE

Imagine you're sitting across from a friend, wanting to share something deeply personal, but there's a lump in your throat, and your palms are sweaty. Welcome to the realm of *vulnerability*, a place where courage and fear do a delicate dance. Vulnerability in communication is about expressing your true feelings, even when they make you feel exposed. It's like allowing others a peek behind the curtain to see the real you, complete with imperfections and insecurities. Far from being a weakness, vulnerability is an act of bravery, inviting authenticity and sincerity into conversations. When you open up, you give permission for others to do the same, creating a ripple effect of genuine dialogue.

The beauty of vulnerability lies in its ability to forge deeper connections. By sharing experiences and emotions, you build bridges of understanding, linking hearts and minds in ways that superficial exchanges cannot. Vulnerability creates a safe space for honesty, where walls crumble, and trust takes root. Imagine a conversation where both parties feel free to express their fears, hopes, and dreams without judgment. It becomes a sanctuary of authenticity, where communication flows freely, and relationships grow stronger. This openness invites a sense of belonging, where individuals feel seen and valued for who they truly are, fostering bonds that withstand the test of time.

So, how do you integrate vulnerability into your everyday conversations? Start by sharing personal stories, those little glimpses into your world that invite empathy and understanding. Whether it's recounting a childhood memory or discussing a recent challenge, sharing your narrative weaves threads of connection. But remember, vulnerability requires boundaries. It's not about oversharing but rather opening up in a way that feels safe and respectful. Set limits to protect your emotional well-being, ensuring that your vulnerability is met with kindness and respect. By balancing openness with self-care, you create an environment where vulnerability thrives, enriching your interactions.

In the workplace, leaders who embrace vulnerability often inspire their teams in remarkable ways. Consider a manager admitting a mistake or expressing uncertainty about a project. This honesty not only humanizes them but also empowers team members to voice their ideas and concerns without fear. Vulnerability becomes a catalyst for innovation, where creativity flourishes, and collaboration reigns. Similarly, personal relationships blossom when vulnerability enters the picture. Imagine a couple navigating a rough patch, choosing to share their fears and insecurities instead of resorting to blame. This openness paves the way for healing and reconciliation, strengthening their bond through mutual understanding.

Take, for instance, a team leader who decides to share their own experiences with burnout, acknowledging the pressure everyone feels. By showing vulnerability, they cultivate a supportive environment where team members are encouraged to discuss their challenges openly. This not only boosts morale but also fosters a sense of unity, as everyone feels part of a collective journey toward well-being. Or envision a friendship rekindled after years of silence, where one person reaches out with an apology and an explanation of past struggles. Their vulnerability opens the door to forgiveness, allowing their relationship to blossom anew with trust and empathy.

5.3 CONFLICT RESOLUTION WITH EMOTIONAL INTELLIGENCE

Imagine a heated discussion in a bustling office, voices rising like popcorn in a microwave. Everyone's talking, but no one's listening, and the tension is thick enough to slice with a butter knife. This is where emotional intelligence steps in, like a skilled conductor bringing *harmony* to a chaotic orchestra. Emotional intelligence offers the tools to identify the underlying issues in any dispute, much like a detective uncovering clues at a mystery scene. By tuning into your emotions and those of others, you can discern the real problems. Maybe it's not about the deadline at all, but a deeper frustration with feeling undervalued. Emotional awareness becomes your compass, guiding you through the maze of conflict to find the root causes hidden beneath the surface.

Empathy, the trusty sidekick of emotional intelligence, plays a crucial role in understanding opposing viewpoints. Imagine seeing a *conflict* from someone else's eyes, like trying on a pair of glasses with a new prescription. Suddenly, their perspective becomes clearer, and what once seemed unreasonable now makes sense. Empathy allows you to step into their shoes, to feel their concerns and motivations, creating a bridge over the chasm of misunderstanding. When you approach conflict with empathy, you open the door to collaboration, where both parties feel heard and respected, setting the stage for resolution.

Effective conflict resolution isn't about winning or losing; it's about finding a path where everyone can walk away feeling satisfied. *Collaborative problem-solving* is your secret weapon, a strategy that turns adversaries into allies. Picture a roundtable discussion where all parties contribute ideas, exploring solutions that benefit everyone. It's like piecing together a jigsaw puzzle, where each person holds a vital piece. Techniques for de-escalating tense situations are also essential. When emotions run high, take a moment to *pause, breathe, and refocus*. This simple act can prevent words from becoming weapons, transforming a heated argument into a constructive conversation.

Communication plays an integral part in resolving conflicts, acting as the glue that holds the resolution process together. Active listening ensures that all voices are heard, fostering an environment of mutual respect. It's like putting on noise-canceling headphones, blocking out distractions to focus on the speaker. Neutral language is your ally here, maintaining objectivity and preventing sparks from igniting into flames. Instead of saying, "You're wrong," try, "I see it differently." This subtle shift in language can make all the difference, keeping the conversation respectful and productive.

Real-world examples abound, demonstrating the power of emotional intelligence in conflict resolution. Consider a workplace dispute between two team members, each convinced they're right. By applying emotional intelligence, they identify the underlying issues, one feels overwhelmed by workload, while the other seeks more recognition. Through empathy and active listening, they find common ground, agreeing to share responsibilities and communicate more openly. In personal settings, imagine a family conflict over holiday plans. With emotional intelligence, family members express their desires and concerns, leading to a compromise that everyone embraces.

5.4 ENHANCING SOCIAL RADAR FOR BETTER INTERACTIONS

Imagine walking into a room and instantly sensing the vibe, whether it's upbeat, tense, or somewhere in between. That's your social radar at work, your internal antenna that picks up on social cues and dynamics. Much like how a skilled radio DJ tunes into the subtle shifts in music to create the perfect playlist, having a keen social radar helps you navigate the complex world of human interactions. It's your ability to read the room, understand unspoken signals, and adapt your communication accordingly. Whether it's noticing a colleague's furrowed brow during a meeting or sensing the excitement of a friend sharing good news, social radar is your guide to more meaningful and effective interactions.

To sharpen your social radar, start with observational exercises. Picture yourself at a café, sipping coffee while people-watching. Notice the body language of those around you, the crossed arms of someone deep in thought or the animated gestures of a lively conversation. Pay attention to the subtleties of facial expressions and tone of voice, as these nonverbal cues often convey more than words alone. Practicing situational awareness in group settings is another valuable strategy. Imagine you're at a networking event, where the ability to read the room can make or break connections. Instead of diving straight into conversations, take a moment to observe the dynamics at play. Who is leading the discussion? Who seems disengaged? This awareness allows you to tailor your approach, ensuring that your interactions are both genuine and effective.

A well-developed social radar can transform your interactions, equipping you with the ability to adapt communication to different social contexts. Think of it as having a universal translator for social settings, allowing you to switch seamlessly between formal and casual, serious and light-hearted. This adaptability fosters stronger relationships, as you become attuned to the needs and emotions of others. In a group dynamic, understanding who needs encouragement or who might benefit from a listening ear enhances your ability to connect on a deeper level. Whether you're navigating a team meeting or a family gathering, a refined social radar helps you engage with authenticity and empathy.

Consider a networking event where your social radar is as sharp as a tack. You notice a fellow attendee standing on the fringes, looking slightly overwhelmed. Instead of sticking with your usual crowd, you approach them, offering a friendly introduction. This simple act, guided by your heightened awareness, leads to a fruitful conversation and a new professional connection. In a team meeting, your social radar helps you navigate group dynamics like a seasoned captain steering a ship. You sense when the conversation is veering off course and gently guide it back, ensuring that everyone's voice is heard. Your ability to read the room fosters collaboration and trust, transforming the meeting into a productive and positive experience.

As we wrap up this chapter on effective communication skills, remember that these abilities are not just tools for interaction but bridges to understanding. By enhancing your emotional literacy, overcoming barriers, embracing vulnerability, resolving conflicts, and fine-tuning your social radar, you equip yourself with a powerful arsenal for personal and professional success. These skills not only enrich your relationships but also empower you to navigate the complexities of human connection with confidence and grace. As we turn the page to explore the next facet of emotional intelligence, consider how you can continue to refine these skills, deepening your understanding of yourself and the world around you.

MAKE A DIFFERENCE, AND PLEASE GIVE A REVIEW

UNLOCK THE POWER OF EMOTIONAL INTELLIGENCE

"We make a living by what we get, but we make a life by what we give."

WINSTON CHURCHILL

Your opinion is powerful!

By sharing your thoughts on *'Emotional Intelligence Decoded'*, you're not just reflecting on your own journey, you're giving others the courage and inspiration to begin theirs.

If this book has helped you gain better understanding of your Emotions and given you tips on how to build ongoing beneficial relationships, your story could be the light that someone else needs to make a change. Every review is a ripple that reaches someone who is ready to grow, succeed and thrive.

Why Your Review Matters:

- **Inspire Others:** Your feedback could be the nudge someone needs to invest in themselves and their future.
- **Share Your Wins:** When you highlight what worked for you, you help others see that success is within their reach.
- **Support the Mission:** Your review spreads the message of the benefits of Emotional Intelligence to more people around the world.

How to Write a Review:

1. **Be Honest:** Share your favorite parts, key takeaways, or how the book made a difference in your life.
2. **Keep It Simple:** A few sentences about what you loved is all it takes to make an impact.
3. **Post It Online:** Reviews on Amazon or Goodreads are the best way to help others discover this guide.

We love helping others and hope you will do the same. Thank you!

Freedom Publications

Scan the QR code to leave your review on Amazon

CHAPTER 6
BUILDING AND SUSTAINING RELATIONSHIPS

Imagine you're at a social gathering, expertly balancing a plate of hors d'oeuvres while engaging in small talk, when a close friend approaches and casually drapes an arm around your shoulder. Friendly, right? But what if that casual touch sends your stress levels through the roof? Welcome to the sometimes tricky world of emotional boundaries. They are like those invisible fences for dogs, except that for humans, they guard our emotional space and well-being. Without these boundaries, relationships can quickly turn into a game of emotional tug-of-war, where one person's needs overshadow the other's. Emotional boundaries are the safeguards that protect your mental health and ensure mutual respect in relationships. They prevent others from trampling over your emotional space and help maintain a sense of identity and autonomy. Think of them as the rules of engagement for emotional interactions, preventing one person from taking the wheel while the other hangs on for dear life.

The importance of emotional boundaries can't be overstated. Establishing healthy boundaries in your relationships is like setting traffic rules; without them, chaos ensues. Imagine a world where everyone respected each other's emotional space as much as they did personal space. You'd have fewer misunderstandings and more room for genuine connection. Healthy boundaries lead to improved communication and understanding, as everyone knows where they stand. They also prevent emotional burnout and resentment, which often arise when boundaries are repeatedly crossed. When you know your limits and communicate them, you protect yourself from taking on more than you can handle, allowing you to engage in relationships without the fear of being overwhelmed or taken for granted.

Setting and maintaining boundaries requires clear communication and consistent action. It's like planting a garden: you need to set the parameters, plant the seeds, and regularly tend to them. Begin by reflecting on what you need from your relationships and what you're willing to tolerate. Communicate these boundaries clearly and assertively, without feeling guilty for doing so. It's okay to say, "I need some time to myself this weekend," or "I can't take on any extra projects right now." The key is to be direct and honest, not leaving room for ambiguity. Once you've set the boundaries, reinforce them through your actions. If someone crosses a line, gently remind them of your boundaries and stand firm. Remember, consistency is crucial; if you let boundaries slide, it sends mixed signals, and others may start to ignore them.

To illustrate this, let's consider some real-world scenarios where boundaries enhance relationship dynamics. In a professional setting, you might set boundaries with colleagues to balance work-life commitments. Imagine a coworker who frequently asks you to cover their shifts. By communicating your limits and sticking to them, you maintain your workload without feeling overwhelmed. In family relationships, boundaries can be a lifesaver. Perhaps you have a family member who drops by unannounced. Politely but firmly express your need for personal space, suggesting scheduled visits instead. These boundaries not only protect your time and energy but also foster healthier, more respectful interactions.

Exercise: Boundary-Setting Reflection

Take a moment to identify a relationship where boundary-setting could improve your well-being. Reflect on what emotional boundaries you need and how you might communicate them assertively. Consider writing down a script for a conversation, outlining your needs clearly and respectfully. Practice this conversation in front of a mirror or with a supportive friend, focusing on maintaining a calm and confident demeanor. Revisit this exercise regularly, adjusting your boundaries as needed to reflect your evolving needs and circumstances.

By setting and maintaining healthy boundaries, you empower yourself to engage in relationships that are both fulfilling and balanced. These boundaries act as your emotional compass, guiding you toward interactions that respect your well-being and foster mutual respect. As you continue to explore the intricacies of emotional intelligence, remember that boundaries are not barriers but bridges to more meaningful connections.

6.1 THE DYNAMICS OF TRUST AND EMPATHY

Imagine trust and empathy as two dancers on the stage of relationships, each moving in harmony to maintain balance. Trust is the sturdy foundation upon which the edifice of empathy is built. Without trust, empathy struggles to find its footing, like a dancer without rhythm. Trust is what allows you to open up, to show vulnerability without fear of judgment or betrayal. It creates a safe space where empathy can flourish, enabling you to truly understand and share another's feelings. On the flip side, empathy is the glue that holds trust together. By empathizing with others, you validate their emotions, reinforcing that trust. They see you as someone who gets them, who listens without preconceived notions, fostering a deeper connection.

Building trust through empathy involves certain steps, akin to a recipe for a delicious dish, where each ingredient is crucial. Start with active listening, which shows you're genuinely invested in understanding others. It's more than hearing words; it's about absorbing the essence of what's being said, acknowledging emotions, and offering support. This act of listening validates the other person's experience, laying the groundwork for trust. Next, consistency is key. Trust isn't built overnight; it requires a series of actions that demonstrate reliability and honesty. Whether it's fulfilling promises or being there in times of need, these consistent actions reinforce trustworthiness, like laying bricks in a solid wall.

The path to building trust isn't always smooth, often strewn with obstacles like past betrayals or cultural differences. Overcoming past breaches of trust can be challenging, akin to rebuilding a bridge after it's been damaged. It requires patience, open communication, and a willingness to work through issues together. Addressing cultural or individual differences in trust perception demands sensitivity and adaptability. Different cultures have varying norms and expectations around trust, and understanding these nuances is crucial. It's about recognizing that what builds trust in one context might differ in another, and being willing to adapt your approach accordingly.

Consider professional partnerships where trust and empathy have paved the way for success. Picture two colleagues from different departments working together on a complex project. By trusting each other's expertise and empathizing with the challenges each faces, they collaborate seamlessly, leading to innovative solutions and a thriving partnership. In personal relationships, empathy can resolve misunderstandings and strengthen bonds. Imagine a couple who, after a heated argument, sit down to listen to each other's perspectives with empathy. By acknowledging each other's feelings and experiences, they find common ground, resolving the conflict and deepening their connection.

In the dance of relationships, trust and empathy move together, supporting and enhancing each other. They are the twin pillars that sustain healthy, meaningful connections, whether in personal or professional settings. As you continue to explore the intricacies of emotional intelligence in relationships, remember the power of trust and empathy to transform and enrich your connections with others.

6.2 RELATIONSHIP BUILDING IN MULTICULTURAL SETTINGS

We live in a multicultural world, and so you may be fortunate enough to meet different people and experience different cultures. Picture this: you're at a global conference, sharing an elevator with a group of colleagues from around the world. Each floor brings new faces, languages, and cultural nuances that are as varied as the elevator music playing softly in the background. This is the vibrant reality of multicultural interactions, where understanding cultural differences becomes your golden ticket to building meaningful relationships. Cultural awareness is like having a universal translator in your pocket, helping you avoid misunderstandings that can often arise when different cultural norms collide. It's the secret ingredient to fostering inclusive environments where everyone feels valued and respected, regardless of their background. By appreciating the unique perspectives each culture brings to the table, you open the door to richer interactions and a deeper understanding of the world around you.

Navigating multicultural settings requires a bit of finesse, but it's not as daunting as it might seem. Start by immersing yourself in cultural norms and values. Think of it as learning the etiquette of a foreign land, where certain gestures or phrases take on different meanings. Whether it's understanding the importance of eye contact or recognizing the significance of personal space, these insights can be game-changers in your interactions. Adapt your communication style to suit diverse backgrounds, like a chameleon adjusting its colors. This might mean speaking more formally or using simpler language, depending on the cultural context. Flexibility and openness are your allies here, allowing you to connect authentically with people from all walks of life.

The benefits of building multicultural relationships are as vast as the diverse cultures they encompass. Engaging with different perspectives broadens your worldview, like adding new lenses to your vision. This diversity enhances creativity, as new ideas and solutions emerge from the fusion of varied experiences. Empathy and adaptability also get a boost as you learn to see the world through the eyes of others, understanding their challenges and triumphs. These skills are invaluable, not just in personal interactions but also in professional settings, where cultural competence is increasingly prized. By embracing multicultural relationships, you cultivate a global mindset that enriches your life and expands your horizons.

Consider a successful international business collaboration where cultural awareness played a pivotal role. Picture a team of professionals from different continents working together on a groundbreaking project. By respecting each other's cultural differences and finding common ground, they create a harmonious environment where innovation thrives. Or imagine a multicultural community project that brings together individuals from diverse backgrounds to address a shared issue. Through open dialogue and mutual respect, they build bridges of understanding, fostering unity and cooperation. These examples highlight the power of cultural awareness to transform interactions, creating spaces where everyone feels heard and valued.

In the dance of multicultural relationships, cultural awareness and sensitivity are your partners, guiding you through the steps with grace and ease. They are the keys to unlocking the potential of diverse interactions, allowing you to connect deeply and authentically with people from all corners of the globe. As you navigate the intricacies of multicultural settings, embrace the richness that diversity brings, and let it inspire you to build relationships that transcend borders and boundaries. Remember, the world is a mosaic of cultures, each piece contributing to the beauty and complexity of the whole.

6.3 EMOTIONAL INTELLIGENCE IN PARENTING

Imagine a quiet Sunday afternoon, where a child's laughter fills the room, but suddenly turns into tears over a toppled LEGO tower. As a parent, your first instinct might be to rebuild the tower for them, but what if instead, you pause, kneel down to their eye level, and ask how they feel? This moment, simple yet profound, is where emotional intelligence steps in, transforming parenting from mere guidance to an empathetic partnership. Emotional intelligence becomes your toolkit for understanding your child's needs, not just hearing their words but truly grasping the emotions behind them. It's about tuning into their world, where a crumbled LEGO tower might feel like the end of the world. This awareness enhances communication within the family, smoothing out the wrinkles of misunderstandings and paving the way for conflict resolution that feels less like a battle and more like a shared discovery of solutions. When you're emotionally attuned to your child's signals, you foster an environment where they feel safe expressing themselves, knowing they'll be met with understanding and support.

The journey to nurturing emotional intelligence in children starts with the most powerful classroom of all, the home. Here, open discussions about emotions take center stage, where feelings are not just acknowledged but welcomed like guests at a family dinner. Transform your living room into a safe space where emotions can be explored without judgment. Encourage your child to talk about their day, sharing not just the events but the emotions tied to them. Ask open-ended questions like, "What was the best part of your day?" or "How did that make you feel?" These conversations teach children to articulate their emotions, building a vocabulary for feelings that will serve them well beyond childhood. Modeling emotional intelligence also plays a crucial role. Children are keen observers, and they learn more from what you do than what you say. When you demonstrate patience during a stressful situation or show empathy towards others, you're teaching them invaluable life skills. They watch how you handle your emotions and mirror your behaviors, finding a template for their own emotional expression.

The impact of emotionally intelligent parenting is significant, shaping children into resilient individuals with strong emotional regulation and social skills. These children grow up with an innate ability to navigate their emotions, approaching life's challenges with a calm demeanor and a sense of confidence. They develop stronger bonds with their parents, built on trust and mutual respect, knowing their feelings are validated and understood. This foundation has ripple effects, extending to their interactions with peers and teachers, where they exhibit empathy and adaptability. They become the kids who help others on the playground, who listen attentively to friends, and who resolve conflicts with a maturity that often surprises adults.

Consider the scenario of managing sibling conflicts, where emotional intelligence shines brightly. Instead of playing referee, you guide your children to articulate their feelings, encouraging them to express why they're upset and what they need from each other. By fostering empathy and understanding, you help them find common ground, transforming squabbles into opportunities for growth. Or take the case of supporting a child through emotional challenges, whether it's the first day of school jitters or the disappointment of not making the soccer team. Your patience and support create a safe harbor, allowing them to weather the storm with resilience. You listen, validate their feelings, and gently guide them toward solutions, teaching them the invaluable lesson that emotions are not to be feared but understood and managed.

In the world of parenting, emotional intelligence is your compass, guiding you through the intricate landscape of raising emotionally healthy children. It's about nurturing their hearts as much as their minds, preparing them to step into the world with empathy, resilience, and a deep understanding of themselves and others.

6.4 EMOTIONAL AGILITY IN FAMILY DYNAMICS

Picture a family as a bustling kitchen full of colorful personalities, each person adding their unique flavor to the mix. Just like in cooking, where you need to adjust the heat and ingredients for the perfect dish, family life requires a similar flexibility to blend all those different personalities harmoniously. This is where emotional agility comes into play. Emotional agility in family dynamics is like having a superpower, allowing each member to adapt to challenges with grace and understanding, rather than getting stuck in unproductive patterns. It's the ability to navigate complex emotions and situations with the same ease as a chef flipping pancakes without letting them hit the floor.

The benefits of emotional agility in families are like the secret sauce that keeps everything running smoothly, even during those inevitable bumps in the road. When family members are emotionally agile, they are better problem solvers, capable of adapting to changing circumstances without losing their cool. Imagine a family vacation where plans fall through due to unexpected weather. Instead of letting frustration take over, an emotionally agile family might quickly pivot to a fun indoor activity, keeping spirits high and avoiding tension. This adaptability lowers stress and enhances communication, reducing misunderstandings that often lead to unnecessary conflicts. It's not about avoiding challenges but about turning them into opportunities for growth and connection.

Developing emotional agility within a family setting involves cultivating a few key practices. Encouraging open dialogue is one of the most effective ways to start. Just as a plant needs sunlight and water to grow, families thrive when everyone's feelings are aired and understood. Create an environment where all voices are heard, where expressing emotions is not only accepted but encouraged. Active listening is crucial here, not just hearing words, but truly understanding the emotions behind them. This practice fosters empathy and strengthens bonds, making it easier to navigate through disagreements or misunderstandings. Another strategy is practicing acceptance and adaptability within family roles. As family dynamics shift, perhaps a child leaving for college or a parent starting a new job, being open to these changes and finding new ways to support each other can prevent resentment and foster a spirit of cooperation.

Consider a family facing a significant life change, such as relocating to a new city. Initially, the thought of leaving familiar surroundings can be daunting. Yet, an emotionally agile family might embrace this change as an adventure, exploring new opportunities together and supporting each other through the transition. Or think of a family where a disagreement arises over household responsibilities. Instead of letting it fester, they might address it with humor and empathy, finding a solution that everyone can agree on. This approach not only resolves the immediate issue but also strengthens the family's ability to handle future challenges together.

In the tapestry of family life, emotional agility is the thread that weaves everything together, creating a fabric that's strong yet flexible, able to withstand the pulls and tugs of daily life. By fostering emotional agility, families can navigate the ups and downs with resilience and understanding, turning challenges into opportunities for deeper connection and growth. As you explore this concept further, consider how you can cultivate emotional agility in your own family, creating a home environment where everyone feels valued, supported, and ready to face whatever comes next.

In essence, emotional agility equips families with the skills to adapt smoothly to life's ever-changing landscape, ensuring harmony and cooperation. With this in mind, we'll soon delve into how emotional intelligence extends beyond immediate family, affecting extended relationships and community interactions.

CHAPTER 7
EMOTIONAL INTELLIGENCE IN LEADERSHIP

Imagine yourself stepping into an office where the energy feels more like a family gathering than a corporate grind. The leader walks in, not with an air of authority that stifles conversation, but with an open demeanor that invites it. This is the power of empathy in leadership, where understanding and supporting team members isn't just a perk, but the essence of what makes a workplace thrive. Empathy, in this context, transcends mere sympathy. It means genuinely stepping into the shoes of your team members, feeling their triumphs, their stresses, and their aspirations. This isn't about offering a sympathetic pat on the back. It's about building a bridge of trust that fosters a supportive environment where team members feel seen and valued.

Empathy as a leadership tool is akin to a master key, unlocking doors to trust and connection that were previously bolted shut. According to research, 80% of senior leaders recognize its importance, but fewer than half of organizations actively practice it. That's like knowing exercise is good for you but choosing to watch workout videos while lounging on the couch. Empathetic leadership enhances personal connections and drives organizational success, transforming workplaces from toxic to vibrant. When leaders truly understand employee emotions, they create spaces where creativity thrives, communication flows, and inclusivity is the norm. It's like nurturing a garden where each plant, or in this case, team member, is given the right conditions to flourish.

The impact of empathetic leadership on team dynamics is profound. It's the difference between a team that drags its feet and one that dances to a harmonious tune. When empathy leads the charge, employee satisfaction skyrockets, and retention follows suit. People don't just work for a paycheck; they stick around because they feel valued and understood. It's like being part of a band where each instrument is appreciated for its unique sound, creating a symphony of collaboration and innovation. Empathetic leadership also acts as a catalyst for creativity. When team members feel safe to express ideas without fear of ridicule, they become more willing to take risks, think outside the box, and propose novel solutions. This freedom to innovate can lead to breakthroughs that propel the entire organization forward.

So, how does one cultivate empathy as a leader? Like any skill, it requires dedication and practice. Start by honing your active listening techniques. This isn't just about nodding along while planning your grocery list; it's about fully engaging with what your team members are saying. Listen not just to respond, but to understand. Reflect back what you've heard, ask clarifying questions, and show genuine interest in their perspectives. Encouraging open communication and feedback is another cornerstone of empathetic leadership. Create an environment where team members feel comfortable sharing their thoughts and concerns, knowing they'll be met with understanding rather than judgment.

Consider the story of a manager who faced a team crisis when a project was unexpectedly canceled. Instead of pointing fingers or issuing ultimatums, the manager gathered the team and asked how they were feeling, encouraging each member to voice their frustrations and fears. By acknowledging their emotions, the manager built a foundation of trust and solidarity. Together, they brainstormed a new direction, and the team emerged stronger, with renewed motivation and camaraderie. This is empathetic leadership in action, transforming potential disaster into opportunity through understanding and support.

One case study that stands out is a tech company where the CEO prioritized empathy as a core leadership value. During a period of rapid growth, the CEO implemented regular check-ins, not just on projects, but on personal well-being. Employees felt heard, and the culture shifted from competitive to collaborative. As a result, the company saw a surge in both employee satisfaction and productivity. Empathy didn't just improve morale; it drove tangible business results, proving that when leaders lead with their hearts, organizations thrive.

7.1 BUILDING EMOTIONALLY INTELLIGENT TEAMS

Imagine a team where everyone communicates openly, trusts each other implicitly, and adapts to change like seasoned dancers adjusting to a new rhythm. This is the hallmark of an emotionally intelligent team, a group that thrives on mutual respect and understanding. Such teams are characterized by high levels of trust and open communication, forming the bedrock of their interactions. When team members trust one another, they're more likely to share ideas freely, collaborate effectively, and support each other through challenges. Open communication ensures that misunderstandings are quickly addressed, and everyone feels heard and valued. It's like having a team where every player knows their role and supports the others, leading to seamless coordination.

In addition to trust and communication, emotionally intelligent teams excel in conflict resolution and adaptability. They possess strong skills in navigating disputes, approaching conflicts not as roadblocks but as opportunities for growth and understanding. This adaptability means that when faced with obstacles, these teams don't crumble; instead, they pivot and find new ways to achieve their goals. It's like watching a group of skilled improvisers who can turn any unexpected twist into an inspiration, keeping the momentum going strong. These characteristics not only enhance team cohesion but also contribute to a more harmonious and productive work environment.

The advantages of cultivating emotional intelligence within teams are manifold. Improved teamwork and reduced interpersonal conflicts lead to a more efficient and enjoyable work atmosphere. When team members understand and regulate their emotions, they're less likely to engage in petty squabbles or hold grudges. Instead, they focus on finding solutions and moving forward. Emotional intelligence also enhances problem-solving and decision-making abilities. Teams that communicate openly and trust one another can tackle complex challenges with creativity and confidence. They draw on diverse perspectives, leveraging each member's strengths to arrive at well-rounded solutions. It's like having a toolbox filled with various tools, each designed to handle a specific task, yet all contributing to the overall success of the project.

To foster emotional intelligence among team members, consider incorporating team-building exercises focused on emotional awareness. These activities encourage individuals to reflect on their emotions and learn how to express them constructively.

Workshops and training sessions on emotional intelligence skills can also be invaluable, providing participants with practical tools and strategies to enhance their interpersonal interactions. These sessions often cover topics such as active listening, empathy, and emotional regulation, equipping team members with the skills needed to navigate the complexities of workplace dynamics. By investing in these initiatives, organizations can create an environment where emotional intelligence is not only encouraged but ingrained in the team's culture.

Take, for example, a project team that faced significant challenges due to tight deadlines and resource constraints. By prioritizing emotional intelligence, they were able to communicate effectively, address conflicts promptly, and support one another through stressful periods. This emotional collaboration allowed them to meet their goals without sacrificing team morale or well-being. Another department that excelled through emotional intelligence was able to achieve high performance by fostering an inclusive and supportive environment. They recognized the diverse strengths of their team members and leveraged these talents to drive innovation and success. These examples illustrate how emotionally intelligent teams can overcome obstacles and achieve remarkable outcomes, demonstrating the power of emotional intelligence in transforming workplace dynamics.

7.2 CONFLICT RESOLUTION IN LEADERSHIP

Imagine you're standing in a room filled with tension so thick you could cut it with a knife. Two team members are at odds, and the atmosphere is like a brewing storm. As a leader, your role is not to point fingers or take sides but to guide the team to clearer skies. Emotional intelligence is your compass in this situation, helping you navigate the storm with deftness and calm. Emotional awareness is your first tool, allowing you to identify the root causes of the conflict rather than just addressing the symptoms. Maybe it's not about who took the last bagel, but rather a feeling of being undervalued or unheard. By recognizing these underlying issues, you're better equipped to address the real problem, not just the surface squabble.

Empathy, another crucial element, allows you to understand the differing perspectives of those involved in the dispute. It's about seeing the conflict through their eyes, understanding why each side feels the way they do. When both parties feel heard and validated, the path to resolution becomes clearer. This doesn't mean you agree with everything, but it does mean you respect their views. Empathy helps you build bridges where walls once stood, turning adversaries into allies. With emotional intelligence, you facilitate discussions that are not about winning or losing but about finding common ground.

As a leader, having structured approaches to conflict resolution can be a game-changer. One such approach is the interest-based relational method, which focuses on identifying the interests behind the positions of each party. It's like peeling an onion, each layer reveals more about what's truly at stake. By concentrating on interests rather than positions, you help team members discover shared goals and mutual benefits. Mediation techniques also play a vital role. Acting as a neutral facilitator, you guide the conversation, ensuring it remains productive and focused on solutions. These techniques transform potentially explosive situations into opportunities for growth and understanding, fostering an environment where differences are not just tolerated but valued.

Proactive conflict management is about anticipating issues before they escalate into full-blown battles. Regular check-ins with your team can act as a pressure release valve, allowing you to gauge tensions and address concerns early. It's like tending to a garden, by nurturing the soil and pulling weeds promptly, you prevent them from overtaking the landscape. Creating a culture of openness also helps. When team members feel comfortable voicing concerns without fear of backlash, conflicts are more likely to be resolved quickly and amicably. This open dialogue nurtures trust and transparency, essential ingredients for a healthy team dynamic.

Consider the story of a leader who turned a divisive conflict into a catalyst for unity. Faced with a team divided over a new project direction, they organized a series of workshops where each member could present their ideas and concerns. By fostering an open exchange, the leader transformed the conflict into a brainstorming session, resulting in a hybrid solution that incorporated the best of both sides. The team emerged not only with a stronger project plan but also with a renewed sense of camaraderie. Another leader faced a similar challenge when two key departments clashed over resource allocation. Instead of issuing a top-down directive, they facilitated a joint meeting where both teams collaborated on a shared strategy, leading to a more efficient use of resources and a stronger interdepartmental relationship.

In these examples, leaders used conflict as a springboard for creativity and collaboration. They showed that with emotional intelligence, what begins as a dispute can become an opportunity for discovery and cohesion. The key lies in approaching conflicts with an open mind, a willingness to listen, and a commitment to finding solutions that respect everyone's interests.

7.3 MOTIVATING AND INSPIRING OTHERS

A good leader doesn't just stand before their team with a list of tasks, but rather with a vision that ignites passion. This is motivation in a leadership context, where emotional intelligence becomes the magic ingredient that turns routine into inspiration. Understanding what drives each team member is crucial. While one person might be fueled by recognition, another may thrive on creative freedom. As a leader, you must tap into these individual and team motivations, aligning them with your organization's goals. It's like syncing your playlist with the perfect soundtrack for a road trip, and when everyone's on the same beat, the journey becomes exhilarating.

Emotionally intelligent motivation isn't just about pep talks and high-fives; it's about creating an environment where engagement and productivity flourish. When leaders craft a space where team members feel genuinely connected to their work, magic happens. Employees become more engaged, productivity surges, and the workplace transforms into a hub of energy and innovation. This isn't just about meeting quotas, it's about sustaining high performance over time. When people are inspired, they don't just clock in and out. They're invested, bringing their best selves to the table day after day. It's the difference between a team that survives and one that thrives.

To effectively motivate and inspire your teams, start by setting clear and attainable goals. It's like plotting a course on a map without a destination, and you risk wandering aimlessly. Clear goals provide a sense of purpose and direction, inspiring action and focus. Celebrate achievements along the way, no matter how small they may seem. Recognition isn't just a pat on the back; it's a powerful motivator that reinforces positive behavior and encourages continued effort. Imagine the impact of acknowledging a team's hard work with a simple yet heartfelt thank you or a public shout-out. These gestures, though small, can have a profound effect on morale and motivation.

Consider the story of a leader who took over a team that had been struggling with low morale and productivity. Instead of cracking the whip, they took the time to understand each team member's aspirations and strengths. By aligning these with the organization's objectives, they reignited a sense of purpose within the team. The leader set clear goals and celebrated every milestone, no matter how minor. As a result, the underperforming team transformed into a powerhouse of creativity and innovation, consistently exceeding expectations. In another example, an organization renowned for its motivational culture encourages leaders to connect with their teams on a personal level, fostering a sense of belonging and shared purpose. By prioritizing motivation and inspiration, these leaders have created an environment where employees are not just workers but enthusiastic contributors to a collective vision.

In these scenarios, leaders use emotional intelligence to elevate motivation from a fleeting feeling to a sustained force. They understand that true inspiration comes from within, and their role is to create the conditions for it to flourish. By recognizing the unique motivations of their team members and aligning them with organizational goals, they unlock a wellspring of potential that drives success.

7.4 NAVIGATING CHANGE WITH EMOTIONAL INTELLIGENCE

Change is one of those words that can send shivers down the spine of even the most seasoned leader. Navigating organizational change is like trying to steer a ship through a storm; it requires skill, patience, and a keen sense of direction. The challenges are many, with resistance to change being a stubborn barnacle on the hull. Team members, comfortable in their routine, may dig in their heels, fearing the unknown more than the status quo. Uncertainty becomes the unwelcome guest at meetings, spreading anxiety as deadlines loom and roles shift. In such times, a leader's resolve is tested, not by how strictly they adhere to plans, but by how gracefully they adapt and lead their team through the choppy waters of transition.

Emotional intelligence becomes the captain's compass, guiding the team through the turbulence of change. Empathy is crucial here, acting as a bridge between leadership and those they lead. It allows leaders to truly hear the concerns of their team, to understand the roots of their resistance, and to address their fears with compassion and clarity. When team members feel understood, they're more likely to step aboard the change train, ready to take the journey together. Emotional regulation, another vital component, ensures that leaders maintain their stability amidst the chaos. By managing their own emotions, leaders can remain a steady presence, instilling confidence and calm in their team.

Leading change effectively is not about issuing edicts from on high; it's about fostering a culture of collaboration and inclusivity. Clear and consistent communication is your best ally. It's like a lighthouse, cutting through the fog of uncertainty, allowing team members to see the path ahead. Share the vision and the reasons behind the change, and do so regularly. Involve team members in the process, inviting their input and valuing their contributions. This inclusion not only increases buy-in but also empowers individuals, making them stakeholders in the journey rather than passive passengers. When people feel they have a say, they're more likely to embrace change and contribute to its success.

Consider a story of a leader at a mid-sized tech firm facing the daunting task of implementing a new software system. Instead of laying down the law, they invited team members to workshops where they could explore the new system together. Questions were encouraged, and feedback was not only welcomed but acted upon. This approach eased anxieties and built a sense of ownership among the team. As a result, the transition was not only smooth but celebrated. Another example is a retail company that had to pivot quickly during an economic downturn. The leadership team prioritized transparency and open dialogue, holding regular meetings to discuss the changes and address concerns. This approach fostered trust and unity, allowing the organization to adapt successfully and emerge stronger.

In these stories, emotionally intelligent leadership transformed potential upheaval into an opportunity for growth and innovation. By prioritizing empathy, emotional regulation, and clear communication, leaders can guide their teams through change with confidence and poise. As we wrap up this chapter on emotional intelligence in leadership, it's clear that these skills are not just nice-to-haves but crucial tools for navigating the complexities of leading people. In the next chapter, we'll explore how emotional intelligence plays a role in personal growth, offering insights and strategies that extend beyond the workplace and into every aspect of life.

CHAPTER 8
EMOTIONAL INTELLIGENCE FOR PERSONAL GROWTH

Picture a child, eyes wide with wonder, stacking colorful blocks to build the tallest tower possible. Each wobble and tumble brings a giggle rather than a groan, as they eagerly try again, adding another block with a steady hand. This simple act captures the essence of a growth mindset, where every challenge is a chance to learn, and every failure is a step closer to success. In the grand theater of personal growth, adopting a growth mindset means believing that your skills and intelligence are not fixed but can be cultivated through effort and perseverance. It's about seeing potential everywhere, even in the things that don't come easily.

Now, let's dive into how this growth mindset beautifully complements emotional intelligence. Emotional intelligence, as we've explored, involves understanding and managing our emotions while navigating social complexities. When paired with a growth mindset, it becomes a dynamic duo that fosters resilience and adaptability. Imagine facing a daunting project at work. Instead of being paralyzed by fear of failure, you see it as a chance to stretch your skills and learn. Emotional intelligence helps you manage the stress and anxiety that might arise, while a growth mindset encourages you to embrace the challenge with open arms. Together, they create a powerful framework for personal development, turning obstacles into opportunities and setbacks into stepping stones.

So, how do you cultivate this growth mindset through emotional intelligence? Start by reframing challenges as opportunities for growth. When faced with a difficult task, remind yourself that every expert was once a beginner. Embrace the discomfort of learning, knowing that each struggle is a sign of progress. Emotional intelligence comes into play here by helping you manage any negative emotions that surface, turning frustration into determination. Another key strategy is to view failures as lessons rather than setbacks. Instead of dwelling on what went wrong, focus on what you can learn from the experience. Emotional intelligence aids in processing these emotions constructively, allowing you to bounce back with renewed vigor. By integrating these approaches, you build a growth mindset that thrives on resilience and adaptability, empowering you to tackle challenges with confidence and creativity.

Combining a growth mindset with emotional intelligence offers a buffet of benefits for personal and professional growth. One delicious dish is increased motivation and persistence in achieving your goals. Imagine you've set a goal to learn a new language. A growth mindset fuels your determination, while emotional intelligence helps you manage the inevitable frustrations of memorizing vocabulary and mastering grammar. Together, they keep you motivated, even when progress feels slow. Another tasty benefit is enhanced problem-solving abilities and creativity. When faced with a complex problem, a growth mindset encourages you to explore multiple solutions, while emotional intelligence helps you navigate the emotions involved, fostering a more creative and innovative approach. This combination not only enriches your personal life but also enhances your professional capabilities, making you a more effective and adaptable leader or team member.

Consider the story of an entrepreneur who exemplifies this blend of growth mindset and emotional intelligence. After several failed business ventures, they could have easily thrown in the towel. Instead, they viewed each failure as a learning experience, analyzing what went wrong and adjusting their approach. Their emotional intelligence helped them manage the stress and disappointment, allowing them to maintain a clear vision and focus on their goals. Eventually, they launched a successful startup that revolutionized their industry, proving that resilience and adaptability are key ingredients for success.

Athletes, too, often embody this powerful combination. Picture a runner who, after countless failed attempts to beat their personal record, finally crosses the finish line with a triumphant smile. They've embraced each setback as an opportunity to refine their technique and improve their performance. Their emotional intelligence helps them manage the pressure and nerves that come with competition, turning each race into a chance to grow and succeed. These stories illustrate how integrating a growth mindset with emotional intelligence can lead to remarkable achievements, inspiring you to harness these principles in your own journey.

Reflection Exercise: Cultivating a Growth Mindset

Think of a recent challenge you faced. Reflect on how you approached it and the emotions involved. Did you see it as an opportunity for growth or a setback? Consider how you might apply a growth mindset and emotional intelligence to similar situations in the future. Write down your thoughts, focusing on how you can embrace challenges and view failures as valuable lessons. This exercise can help you develop a more resilient and adaptable mindset, empowering you to navigate life's challenges with confidence and creativity.

8.1 OVERCOMING THE INNER CRITIC

Imagine you have a constant companion who whispers doubts into your ear, questioning every decision and critiquing every action. This, my friend, is your inner critic, a relentless voice that thrives on self-doubt and negative self-talk. It's the part of you that raises an eyebrow when you dare to dream big or tries to shush your creativity with a "that's impossible." The inner critic can be a formidable foe, limiting your potential and stifling the creative spark that makes you unique. It's like having an overly critical movie reviewer sitting in your brain, pointing out flaws in every scene of your life. This critic can leave you second-guessing yourself, making you hesitate when you should leap and whispering "not good enough" when you try to celebrate your accomplishments.

Silencing this inner critic requires a bit of strategy and a hefty dose of self-compassion. The first step is to recognize and challenge those pesky negative thought patterns. When your mind starts to spiral with self-doubt, pause and ask yourself, is this thought based on fact or fear? Often, these critical voices are echoes of past insecurities rather than truths about your abilities. Next, practice self-compassion exercises to foster a kinder, more supportive inner dialogue. Imagine speaking to yourself as you would a dear friend, offering encouragement instead of criticism. This might feel odd at first, but self-love can be a rebellious act in a world that thrives on comparison, but it's a powerful way to shift your mindset. By replacing harsh judgments with understanding, you create a mental space where your true potential can flourish.

Emotional intelligence provides a valuable toolkit for managing self-critical thoughts. Using self-awareness, you can identify the triggers that set your inner critic into overdrive. Perhaps it's a particular situation, like a challenging project at work, or a specific person, like a critical family member. Recognizing these triggers allows you to prepare and respond with emotional intelligence rather than getting swept away by negativity. Additionally, emotional intelligence helps you navigate these thoughts with grace, turning what could be an emotional pitfall into an opportunity for growth. By understanding your emotional patterns, you can develop strategies to counteract the critic's influence, empowering you to forge a path toward self-belief and confidence.

To strengthen self-confidence and reduce self-doubt, try incorporating daily affirmations into your routine. These positive statements can reinforce a healthier self-perception, reminding you of your strengths and accomplishments. Consider starting your day by looking in the mirror and stating affirmations like, "I am capable, I am resilient, and I am worthy." It might feel a bit cheesy at first, but these affirmations can act as a powerful antidote to negativity, much like a dose of sunshine on a cloudy day. Additionally, journaling exercises focused on personal achievements can help shift your focus from what you haven't done to what you have. Create a "Wins Journal" where you jot down even the smallest victories, whether it's completing a task you've been putting off or simply getting through a tough day. Reflecting on these achievements can boost your confidence and remind you of your ability to overcome challenges.

In a world that often seems eager to point out flaws, managing your inner critic with emotional intelligence is a transformative act of self-love. By practicing self-awareness, self-compassion, and positive reinforcement, you can quiet that critical voice and allow your true potential to shine. It's about creating an inner dialogue that supports rather than sabotages, nurturing a mindset that celebrates growth and learning over perfection. As you navigate the complexities of personal growth, remember that you have the power to shape your inner narrative, transforming self-doubt into self-belief and negativity into empowerment.

8.2 EMOTIONAL INTELLIGENCE AND PERSONAL FULFILLMENT

If you could wake up each morning with a sense of purpose, feeling that your actions align with your deepest values, wouldn't that be fantastic? Personal fulfillment is that elusive yet deeply satisfying state where you feel content and purposeful in your life. It's about more than just checking off boxes on a to-do list; it's about living a life that resonates with who you truly are. Emotional intelligence plays a crucial role in this pursuit by helping you understand what truly matters to you and how to make decisions that reflect those values. It's like having an internal compass that guides your actions, ensuring that you're not just going through the motions but living with intention and satisfaction.

Achieving personal fulfillment through emotional intelligence involves setting goals that are not just ambitious but meaningful. These goals should speak to the core of who you are, reflecting your passions and values. For instance, if you value creativity, setting a goal to start a new art project or learn an instrument can bring a sense of fulfillment. Emotional intelligence aids in this process by helping you tune into your emotions and recognize what genuinely excites and fulfills you. Another strategy is cultivating gratitude, which shifts your focus from what you lack to appreciating the richness of your experiences. Regularly reflecting on what you're grateful for can enhance your emotional well-being and deepen your sense of fulfillment.

The pursuit of personal fulfillment through emotional intelligence leads to a more enriching life. When you align your actions with your values, you experience increased happiness and life satisfaction. You're no longer chasing after external markers of success but focusing on what truly brings you joy. This alignment fosters stronger relationships, as you attract and connect with people who share your values and support your journey. You're more present in your interactions, more compassionate and understanding, because you're operating from a place of authenticity. This authenticity strengthens your bonds with others, creating a supportive network that enhances your fulfillment.

Consider a professional who found fulfillment by aligning their career with their passions. After years of feeling uninspired in a corporate job, they decided to pursue a career in environmental advocacy, a field they'd always been passionate about. This shift was challenging, requiring them to tap into their emotional intelligence to manage the fears and uncertainties that arose. However, the result was a career that not only fulfilled them but also made a meaningful impact on the world. Their story illustrates how aligning your actions with your values through emotional intelligence can lead to profound personal fulfillment.

On a more personal level, think of individuals who transformed their lives by embracing authenticity. One such person may have always felt pressured to follow a traditional path, perhaps pursuing a career or lifestyle that didn't resonate with their true self. By using emotional intelligence to explore their genuine interests and passions, they began living authentically, making choices that reflected their true identity. This shift brought a profound sense of fulfillment, as they were finally living a life true to themselves. Their relationships improved as well, as they were able to connect with others on a deeper, more genuine level.

Personal fulfillment is not a destination but an ongoing process, a series of choices and actions that align with who you are. By leveraging emotional intelligence, you can navigate this process with clarity and purpose, ensuring that your life is not just filled with activities but with meaning and satisfaction. In doing so, you create a life that feels rich and fulfilling, one where each day brings new opportunities for growth and joy.

8.3 EMOTIONAL INTELLIGENCE AND MENTAL HEALTH

Imagine your mind as a bustling city, with emotions zipping around like busy commuters. In this vibrant metropolis, emotional intelligence acts like a skilled traffic controller, ensuring everything runs smoothly, even during rush hour. Emotional intelligence is a powerful ally in maintaining mental health, acting as a buffer against the stress and anxiety that often accompany life's challenges. It's like having an internal GPS that reroutes you around emotional gridlocks, helping you navigate the complexities of daily life with ease.

When stress and anxiety threaten to overwhelm, emotional intelligence steps in as a reliable coping mechanism. Enhancing emotional resilience empowers you to bounce back from setbacks and adapt to new situations. This resilience is crucial for mental well-being, as it allows you to face life's inevitable ups and downs with confidence. Emotional intelligence helps you identify and manage your emotions, preventing them from spiraling out of control. It's like having an emotional toolkit, equipped with strategies to handle whatever life throws your way.

One strategy for using emotional intelligence to improve mental health is mindfulness. This practice involves paying attention to the present moment, without judgment, allowing you to become more aware of your thoughts and feelings. By embracing mindfulness, you can enhance your emotional awareness and regulation, creating a sense of calm and clarity. Imagine being able to pause and observe your emotions as they arise, rather than getting swept away by them. Mindfulness helps you do just that, acting as a mental anchor in turbulent times.

Building supportive relationships is another powerful way to leverage emotional intelligence for mental well-being. These connections provide a sense of belonging and emotional support, acting as a safety net when you need it most. By cultivating empathy and understanding, you can strengthen your relationships, creating a network of support that fosters mental health. Think of your relationships as a garden that thrives when nurtured with care and attention. Emotional intelligence helps you cultivate these connections, ensuring they flourish even in challenging times.

The importance of emotional intelligence in preventing mental health issues cannot be overstated. By identifying and addressing emotional triggers before they escalate, you can prevent stress and anxiety from taking hold. Imagine having a radar that detects emotional storm clouds on the horizon, allowing you to take shelter before the storm hits. Emotional intelligence offers this radar, helping you navigate life's challenges with foresight and preparation.

Consider the story of an individual who used emotional intelligence to improve their mental health. After struggling with depression, they began practicing mindfulness and building supportive relationships. These strategies helped them develop emotional resilience, enabling them to manage their emotions more effectively. Over time, they experienced a significant improvement in their mental well-being, illustrating the transformative power of emotional intelligence.

Another example is someone who managed anxiety through emotional regulation techniques. By using mindfulness and self-awareness, they learned to identify their anxiety triggers and respond with calm and clarity. This approach allowed them to regain control over their emotions, reducing the impact of anxiety on their daily life. Their story highlights how emotional intelligence can act as a protective factor, preventing mental health issues and promoting overall well-being.

In the hustle and bustle of life, emotional intelligence stands as a beacon of stability, guiding you through the complexities of mental health. By embracing mindfulness, building supportive relationships, and addressing emotional triggers, you can enhance your mental well-being and create a life filled with resilience and fulfillment. Whether you're navigating stress, anxiety, or life's unexpected challenges, emotional intelligence equips you with the tools to thrive.

8.4 HARNESSING EMOTIONAL STRENGTHS FOR SUCCESS

Imagine walking into a room and instantly feeling the energy shift. You sense the mood, the dynamics, without anyone saying a word. That's the power of emotional strengths, those innate attributes that allow you to navigate the world with a keen sense of awareness and empathy. Emotional strengths are the personal qualities that enhance your performance, whether it's the ability to remain calm under pressure, the knack for inspiring others, or the gift of truly understanding what someone else is feeling. They're like your emotional superpowers, quietly working behind the scenes to boost your effectiveness in both personal and professional settings.

Identifying these strengths can be a game-changer. It starts with self-assessment exercises that shine a light on your core emotional competencies. Take a moment to reflect on situations where you've thrived or felt particularly capable. What emotions were at play? Were you using your empathy to connect with others, or your emotional regulation to steer through stress? Once you've pinpointed your strengths, the next step is setting goals that align with and leverage these attributes. If you're a natural communicator, consider roles or projects that allow you to use this skill. Aligning your goals with your emotional strengths not only amplifies success but also brings a sense of fulfillment and authenticity to your endeavors.

The benefits of leveraging emotional strengths are multifaceted. In a professional context, they can lead to enhanced leadership and teamwork abilities. A leader who harnesses empathy and emotional regulation can inspire a team, even in challenging times, creating an environment where ideas flourish and collaboration thrives. These strengths also boost self-efficacy and confidence. When you know your emotional strengths and use them wisely, you move through life with a grounded assurance, ready to tackle obstacles and seize opportunities.

Consider the story of a leader who excelled by leveraging their emotional strengths. Known for their empathy and emotional regulation, they led their team through a major organizational change. While others might have been overwhelmed, this leader maintained a steady course, listening to concerns and providing support. Their calm demeanor and genuine understanding fostered trust, enabling the team to adapt and innovate. Another example is an entrepreneur who thrived by harnessing their passion and resilience. After facing initial setbacks, they channeled their emotional strengths into a venture that aligned with their values, ultimately achieving success that resonated deeply with them.

These stories illustrate the transformative power of emotional strengths. By understanding and utilizing these attributes, you can navigate the complexities of life with greater ease and effectiveness. Whether you're leading a team, building a business, or simply seeking personal growth, emotional strengths provide the foundation for success. They enhance your ability to connect with others, adapt to change, and pursue goals that truly matter. As you continue to explore and develop your emotional intelligence, remember that these strengths are your allies, ready to support and guide you on your path.

CHAPTER 9
OVERCOMING BARRIERS AND OBJECTIONS

Imagine stepping into a bustling marketplace, where each stall represents a different aspect of emotional intelligence. As you wander through, you overhear snippets of a conversation, "Isn't emotional intelligence just about being overly emotional?" or "I thought you either had it or you didn't." These misconceptions linger like persistent myths, clouding our understanding of what emotional intelligence truly entails. Let's dive into these myths and clear the air, because once you peel back the layers, you'll find that emotional intelligence is as much about skill as it is about emotion.

One of the most common misconceptions is the idea that emotional intelligence is something you're simply born with, as if it's an innate trait like eye color or a penchant for pineapple on pizza. This belief can be discouraging, leading many to think that improving their emotional intelligence is futile. However, emotional intelligence is not set in stone. Think of it like learning to play an instrument. Just as you can learn to strum a guitar or tickle the piano keys with practice and dedication, you can develop and enhance your emotional intelligence over time. Dr. Daniel

Goleman, who popularized the concept, emphasized that emotional intelligence involves a range of skills, like self-control and empathy, that can be cultivated with effort and commitment (Source: LID Publishing).

Another myth that often crops up is the notion that emotional intelligence equates to being overly emotional, like a character in a soap opera throwing dramatic tantrums. This couldn't be further from the truth. Emotional intelligence is about balanced emotional expression. It's the ability to understand and manage your emotions while empathizing with others, not letting emotions run riot like a toddler in a candy store. It's about finding that sweet spot between feeling and thinking, so you can navigate life's challenges with poise and clarity. Emotional intelligence involves a set of emotional and social skills that help you influence others and manage relationships effectively, think of it as your emotional Swiss Army knife, handy in any situation.

These myths can seriously hinder personal growth. If you believe emotional intelligence is innate or purely emotional, you might shy away from embracing it, thinking it's either impossible or undesirable to develop. This reluctance can hold you back from reaching your full potential, both personally and professionally. After all, emotional intelligence plays a significant role in financial and personal success, as highlighted by research from the Carnegie Institute of Technology, which found that 85% of financial success is due to skills in 'human engineering'—an area where emotional intelligence shines (Source: LID Publishing).

So, how do we overcome these misconceptions and embrace a more accurate understanding of emotional intelligence? Education is key. By accessing resources that promote awareness and understanding, you can demystify emotional intelligence and see it for what it truly is: a valuable skill set that enhances your life.

Consider reading books, attending workshops, or exploring online courses that delve into emotional intelligence. These resources can offer insights into the practical application of emotional intelligence in daily life, from managing stress to building stronger relationships.

Reflection Exercise: Spotting Myths in Your Life

Take a moment to reflect on how you perceive emotional intelligence. Have any of these myths influenced your understanding or willingness to develop this skill? Jot down any preconceived notions you might have had and consider how they might have impacted your personal growth. Then, explore resources or seek conversations that challenge these myths, opening the door to a more informed perspective on emotional intelligence.

By debunking these myths and embracing emotional intelligence as a learned and balanced skill, you're setting the stage for personal growth and success. You empower yourself to navigate your emotions and relationships with greater understanding and effectiveness.

9.1 TIME MANAGEMENT FOR PERSONAL DEVELOPMENT

Balancing personal development with daily responsibilities can feel like juggling flaming torches while riding a unicycle on a tightrope. In a world that never seems to slow down, managing your time effectively becomes crucial, especially when it comes to nurturing your emotional intelligence. It's not just about cramming more into your day; it's about prioritizing what truly matters and creating space for growth amidst the chaos. Emotional intelligence thrives on reflection and practice, but finding time for these can be as elusive as finding a quiet spot in a bustling café.

So, how do you make time for emotional intelligence when your schedule is already bursting at the seams? Start by setting aside dedicated time for self-reflection and mindfulness practices. Think of it as scheduling a meeting with yourself. Whether it's a quiet moment with your morning coffee or a few minutes of deep breathing before bed, these pockets of time can make a world of difference. They allow you to tune into your emotions and reflect on your interactions, laying the groundwork for emotional growth. Additionally, technology can be your ally in this endeavor. There are apps designed to remind and track your emotional intelligence activities, nudging you gently when life gets in the way. These digital companions can help you stay consistent, transforming emotional development into a daily habit rather than a fleeting thought.

The benefits of effective time management extend far beyond mere organization. When you manage your time well, you create a nurturing environment for your emotional intelligence to flourish. Consistency in practicing emotional intelligence skills leads to deeper self-awareness and improved relationships. It becomes easier to recognize emotional patterns and respond thoughtfully rather than react impulsively. Imagine consistently setting aside time each week to journal about your emotions and experiences. Over time, you'll notice patterns and triggers, equipping you with insights to manage your responses more effectively. It's like training for a marathon; each practice session builds endurance and strength, preparing you for the emotional challenges life throws your way.

Consider the stories of individuals who have successfully integrated emotional intelligence practices into their busy lives. Take, for instance, a professional whose workday is filled with meetings, emails, and deadlines. By carving out a few minutes each morning for mindfulness meditation, they find clarity and focus, approaching tasks with a calm mind. Their emotional intelligence becomes their secret weapon, enabling them to navigate workplace dynamics with empathy and understanding. Or consider a parent juggling the demands of work, family, and personal growth. They dedicate time for self-reflection during their child's nap, using this quiet moment to recharge and reflect. This practice not only enhances their emotional intelligence but also enriches their interactions with their family, fostering a nurturing environment for growth.

Effective time management is not about squeezing more into your day but about making room for what truly matters. By prioritizing emotional intelligence, you invest in your personal growth and well-being. You become more attuned to your emotions, more empathetic in your interactions, and more resilient in the face of challenges. It's about finding balance amidst the busyness, allowing your emotional intelligence to thrive.

9.2 PERSONALIZED STRATEGIES FOR EMOTIONAL GROWTH

Think of emotional growth like a garden. Each garden is unique, with different plants needing specific care. Similarly, emotional growth thrives on personalized approaches. One-size-fits-all strategies rarely work because we all come with our own set of emotional experiences and needs. What works for your friend might not suit you at all. This is why understanding your own emotional landscape is crucial. You have unique strengths and areas where you could use a little more nurturing. Maybe you're excellent at empathizing with others but struggle with self-regulation when stressed. Recognizing these individual traits allows you to tailor your approach to developing emotional intelligence in a way that resonates with you personally.

Creating a personalized emotional growth plan begins with identifying your personal emotional strengths and areas for improvement. It's like taking stock of your garden, noting which plants are thriving and which ones need more sunlight or water. Start by reflecting on your past experiences and interactions. What emotional skills are you proud of? Maybe you excel at listening but find it hard to express your own needs. Understanding these nuances helps you set specific, achievable goals for your emotional development. Just as you wouldn't try to grow a cactus in a swamp, you shouldn't aim for goals that don't align with your natural tendencies or circumstances. Set realistic objectives that challenge you but are attainable, fostering a sense of accomplishment and motivation.

Self-assessment is your compass in this journey, guiding your personal development efforts. Use self-assessment tools to track your progress and adjust strategies as needed. These tools act like a gardener's notebook, providing insights into what's working and what needs tweaking. Regularly assess your emotional responses and interactions, noting patterns and changes over time. This self-awareness allows you to celebrate your progress and address any setbacks with a constructive mindset. Think of it as a feedback loop; each assessment offers valuable information that informs your next steps, enabling you to refine your approach and continue growing emotionally.

Consider the story of Sam, a young professional who wanted to improve his emotional intelligence to enhance his leadership skills. Sam recognized his strength in motivating his team, but grappled with managing stress during high-pressure situations. By creating a personalized growth plan, he set specific goals to enhance his self-regulation and stress management skills. He incorporated mindfulness practices into his daily routine and sought feedback from colleagues to gauge his progress. Over time, Sam noticed a significant improvement in handling stress and maintaining composure, which positively impacted his professional relationships and team dynamics. Sam's journey highlights the power of personalized approaches, demonstrating how tailored strategies can lead to meaningful growth and success.

Another example is Lisa, a mother balancing work and family life. She realized her emotional intelligence needed a boost, particularly in expressing her needs without feeling guilty. Lisa crafted a growth plan focusing on assertive communication and setting boundaries. She attended workshops and practiced role-playing with a friend to reinforce these skills. Gradually, Lisa noticed a transformation in her relationships, both at home and work. She felt more confident in expressing her needs and experienced less emotional burnout. Her personalized approach not only improved her emotional intelligence but also enhanced her overall well-being and connection with loved ones.

Personalized strategies for emotional growth empower you to take charge of your development, aligning your efforts with your unique qualities and circumstances. By embracing your individuality, setting specific goals, and using self-assessment to guide your path, you cultivate a more authentic and effective approach to emotional intelligence. This tailored method ensures that your growth is not only meaningful but also sustainable, allowing you to flourish in all areas of your life.

Interactive Learning: Beyond the Book

Imagine learning emotional intelligence as not just reading about it, but actually living it. That's where interactive learning comes into play. Instead of passively flipping through pages, you're actively engaging with the material, making it stick like glue. This approach turns learning into a dynamic experience, capturing your attention and making the concepts more memorable. Interactive learning methods have revolutionized how we approach emotional intelligence, providing practical, hands-on experiences that transform abstract ideas into tangible skills. Picture a workshop where you're not just listening to a lecture, but participating in role-playing exercises that put your empathy and communication skills to the test. Suddenly, emotional intelligence isn't just a concept, it's a skill you're actively developing.

Workshops and seminars specifically focused on emotional intelligence are powerful tools in this interactive arsenal. They offer a space to practice new skills in real-time, with guidance and feedback from experienced facilitators. Imagine a room full of people, each with their own emotional intelligence goals, working together to break down barriers and build stronger connections. Through guided activities and discussions, these settings create a supportive environment where you can explore your emotional landscape without judgment. Role-playing exercises, in particular, allow you to step into someone else's shoes, fostering empathy by experiencing different perspectives. It's like a dress rehearsal for real-life interactions, preparing you to navigate complex social situations with greater ease.

Then there are online courses, which have embraced interactive elements to enhance learning even further. These courses often include quizzes, discussions, and interactive scenarios that challenge you to apply what you've learned. Picture logging into an online platform, where you're greeted with an engaging module on emotional awareness. As you progress, you're prompted to reflect on real-life experiences, participate in discussions with peers, and complete quizzes that reinforce key concepts. The beauty of these courses is their flexibility, allowing you to learn at your own pace while still reaping the benefits of interactive engagement. They're perfect for those who prefer a more structured approach to learning, with the added bonus of being accessible from anywhere.

The benefits of interactive learning for emotional growth are profound. For starters, the engaging formats keep you motivated to practice emotional intelligence skills regularly. When learning is fun and interactive, you're more likely to stick with it, incorporating the lessons into your daily life. This consistency is key to building and maintaining emotional intelligence, as it reinforces neural pathways and strengthens your abilities over time. Moreover, interactive learning fosters a deeper understanding of emotional concepts, as you're actively participating in the learning process rather than passively absorbing information. It's the difference between reading about swimming and actually diving into the water; one gives you knowledge, while the other gives you skill.

Consider the story of a participant in an emotional intelligence workshop who entered with a vague understanding of the topic and left with newfound clarity and confidence. Through peer feedback and interactive activities, they identified their emotional strengths and areas for improvement, equipping them with tools to navigate personal and professional relationships more effectively. Or think of an online learner who discovered insights into their emotional patterns through engaging course materials. By participating in discussions and completing interactive exercises, they gained a deeper understanding of their emotions, leading to significant personal growth and enhanced emotional intelligence. These experiences highlight the transformative power of interactive learning, showcasing its ability to bring emotional intelligence concepts to life in meaningful ways.

Interactive learning bridges the gap between theory and practice, offering a dynamic approach to emotional intelligence development that is both engaging and effective. Whether through workshops, role-playing exercises, or online courses, these methods provide valuable opportunities to actively cultivate emotional intelligence skills, fostering personal growth and enriching your interactions with others.

9.3 OVERCOMING SKEPTICISM WITH PRACTICAL RESULTS

In a world brimming with self-help books and life coaches promising the moon, it's no wonder some folks raise an eyebrow when emotional intelligence enters the conversation. There's a lingering skepticism about its practicality and whether it truly delivers on its promises. Some people wonder if emotional intelligence is just another trendy buzzword, with concepts that sound good in theory but fall flat when the rubber meets the road. This doubt often stems from a misunderstanding of how emotional intelligence works in real-life scenarios. For those who equate emotional intelligence with being overly touchy-feely, it might seem like a skill set better suited for therapists than for the average person navigating daily life.

Let's set those doubts aside for a moment and focus on the hard evidence. Research consistently shows that emotional intelligence can lead to remarkable improvements in job performance. Studies have found that individuals with higher emotional intelligence tend to excel in the workplace, as they navigate complex interpersonal dynamics and adapt to changing environments with ease. A study conducted by the Carnegie Institute of Technology concluded that 85% of financial success is due to skills in 'human engineering,' which includes emotional intelligence. This research emphasizes that emotional awareness and the ability to empathize with others are key components of professional success. Take, for instance, a manager who used emotional intelligence to transform a disengaged team into a cohesive, high-performing unit. By understanding the emotions and motivations of team members, the manager created an environment where everyone felt valued and heard, leading to improved productivity and morale.

Beyond the workplace, emotional intelligence can trigger profound personal transformations. I've seen individuals who once struggled with self-doubt and relationship challenges turn their lives around by developing emotional intelligence skills. One person I know found that by honing their ability to manage emotions, they gained newfound confidence and improved their relationships with family and friends. By learning to respond thoughtfully rather than react impulsively, they created a more harmonious and fulfilling personal life. These stories and studies paint a vivid picture of the tangible benefits emotional intelligence can offer, dispelling any lingering skepticism about its impact.

To truly appreciate the value of emotional intelligence, it's helpful to set clear goals and track progress in developing emotional skills. By identifying specific areas for improvement, such as empathy or emotional regulation, and measuring progress over time, you can see the incremental changes that add up to significant growth. Sharing testimonials and success stories with others can also inspire confidence and highlight the positive impact emotional intelligence can have. These real-world examples showcase how emotional intelligence can lead to stronger relationships, better mental health, and increased professional success.

Consider the story of a business leader who transformed their company culture through emotional intelligence. By prioritizing employee well-being and fostering open communication, they created an environment where innovation and collaboration thrived. The results were clear, increased employee satisfaction, reduced turnover, and a more resilient organization. On a personal level, I've witnessed friends leverage emotional intelligence to navigate life changes with grace, whether transitioning careers or overcoming personal challenges. These examples demonstrate that emotional intelligence isn't just a theoretical concept; it's a practical skill that can lead to positive change.

In this chapter, we've explored how emotional intelligence can break down barriers, dispel skepticism, and drive personal and professional growth. Emotional intelligence isn't just a passing fad; it's a valuable tool that helps you navigate the complexities of life with empathy and resilience. As we move forward, we'll delve into the next chapter, where we'll explore how to apply these insights more effectively in real-world scenarios, enhancing both your personal and professional relationships.

CHAPTER 10
APPLYING EMOTIONAL INTELLIGENCE IN REAL LIFE

Imagine yourself walking into the office on a Monday morning, coffee in hand, only to find your team huddled around the water cooler, whispering about last week's email debacle. You know the one, the email sent accidentally to the entire company instead of just your supervisor. Oops! Now, here's where emotional intelligence, if used correctly, can save the day. Emotional intelligence used appropriately and correctly in the workplace can transform awkward situations into opportunities for growth and understanding. It's not just about putting out fires, it's about preventing them in the first place.

Emotional intelligence plays a crucial role in professional success, acting as the glue that holds teams together and propels individuals forward in their careers. When we talk about EQ in the workplace, we're looking at a blend of self-awareness, empathy, and social skills that create a harmonious environment. Leaders with high emotional intelligence are like skilled conductors, guiding their teams with empathy and understanding. They don't just bark orders, they listen, adapt, and inspire. This fosters an atmosphere where employees feel valued, ultimately boosting engagement and productivity. According to the Center for Creative Leadership, high emotional intelligence in leaders is linked to greater employee engagement and organizational profitability.

Incorporating emotional intelligence into your daily work routine can be as simple as practicing empathy during team meetings. Imagine a meeting where everyone talks over each other, resulting in chaos and confusion. Now picture a different scenario, where you listen actively, acknowledging each person's contributions and concerns. By fostering inclusivity, you create a space where ideas flow freely, and collaboration thrives. Similarly, using emotional regulation to handle workplace stress effectively can make a world of difference. Instead of allowing stress to spiral out of control, you take a moment to breathe, recalibrate, and approach challenges with a calm, composed mindset.

Consider the power of emotional intelligence in resolving workplace conflicts. Imagine a manager who navigates a tense situation between two team members. Instead of taking sides, they employ empathetic communication to understand each person's perspective, creating a dialogue that leads to a resolution. This approach not only resolves the conflict but also strengthens the team's cohesion. In another scenario, an employee uses their emotional awareness to enhance customer relationships. They pick up on subtle cues, such as a customer's tone or body language, and respond with empathy, transforming a potentially negative interaction into a positive experience.

Emotional intelligence isn't just a tool for diffusing tension, it's a catalyst for career advancement. In today's competitive job market, emotional intelligence sets you apart. It's the differentiator that employers seek, recognizing its value in fostering strong interpersonal relationships and effective leadership. High emotional intelligence can lead to professional growth and opportunities that might have otherwise remained elusive. Success stories abound of individuals who have climbed the career ladder thanks to their emotional intelligence. Their ability to connect with others, manage emotions, and adapt to changing circumstances positions them as leaders in their fields.

Case Study: Emotional Intelligence in Action

Let's take a look at Sarah, a project manager at a bustling tech startup. Sarah was known for her technical prowess, but it was her emotional intelligence that truly set her apart. During a critical project, tensions ran high as deadlines loomed. Sarah noticed the stress levels rising and decided to hold a team meeting focused on emotional well-being. She encouraged team members to share their concerns and feelings, fostering a supportive atmosphere. As a result, the team felt heard and valued, and productivity soared. Sarah's empathetic leadership style earned her a promotion, highlighting the impact of emotional intelligence on career advancement.

In another example, consider Tom, a customer service representative at a busy call center. Tom excelled at his job because he didn't just address customer complaints; he connected with them emotionally. He listened actively, empathized with their frustrations, and provided solutions that resonated with their needs. His ability to understand and manage emotions led to higher customer satisfaction rates and glowing reviews. Tom's dedication to emotional intelligence resulted in recognition from his superiors and opened doors to new opportunities within the company.

Emotional intelligence isn't just a buzzword; it's a vital component of professional success. By embracing its principles, you can navigate the complexities of the workplace with confidence and grace.

Whether you're leading a team, collaborating with colleagues, or interacting with customers, emotional intelligence empowers you to build meaningful connections, resolve conflicts, and seize new opportunities.

10.1 NAVIGATING MAJOR LIFE TRANSITIONS

Imagine standing at the edge of a diving board, looking down at the pool below, knowing that the plunge will be exhilarating yet daunting. Major life transitions can feel a lot like this. Whether you're leaping into a new career, moving to a new city, or finding your footing as a new parent, these changes bring with them a whirlwind of emotions. There's excitement, sure, but there's also anxiety, uncertainty, and sometimes a sprinkle of fear. Career changes, for instance, can leave you feeling unmoored, questioning your identity and your place in the world. Relocation might promise adventure, but it also means leaving behind the familiar comforts of home. Then there's the shift in family dynamics, a new marriage, the arrival of a child, or even an empty nest, all of which can stir a complex mix of joy and trepidation. These transitions challenge us to adapt, to reshape our lives and redefine our roles, often leaving us feeling overwhelmed.

So, how can emotional intelligence ease the rollercoaster ride of life changes? First, set realistic expectations and goals. Think of it as mapping out your journey with a trusty GPS. Instead of expecting perfection, acknowledge that there will be bumps along the way. A career change might not lead to instant success, and settling into a new home might take longer than expected. By setting achievable goals, you give yourself the grace to grow and adapt at your own pace. Building a support network is equally important. Surround yourself with friends, family, or even a mentor who can offer guidance and a listening ear. They can provide the emotional stability you need when the going gets tough. Remember, it's okay to lean on others when you're navigating uncharted waters. Emotional intelligence also involves self-regulation, that is, keeping your emotions in check and preventing them from derailing your progress. When anxiety creeps in, practice mindfulness or deep breathing to ground yourself in the present moment.

Consider the story of Alex, who recently transitioned from a bustling corporate job to a quieter life as a freelance writer. Initially, the change felt liberating but soon gave way to feelings of isolation and doubt. However, by setting small, achievable goals, like completing one article a week, Alex found structure in the chaos. Building a network of fellow freelancers provided much-needed camaraderie and support, helping Alex navigate the ups and downs of self-employment. Similarly, the Johnson family faced a significant transition when they adopted a child. The new family dynamics brought joy, but also challenges. By using emotional intelligence to empathize with each other's needs and emotions, they strengthened their bonds during this transformative period. Weekly family meetings became a safe space for open communication, allowing each member to express their feelings and adjust to their new roles.

Applying emotional intelligence during life transitions can profoundly impact your well-being. Imagine feeling less anxious and more confident as you navigate these changes. Emotional intelligence empowers you to approach transitions with a sense of calm and resilience. It enhances your adaptability, allowing you to pivot and problem-solve effectively when faced with unexpected obstacles. As you cultivate these skills, you become better equipped to handle whatever life throws your way, transforming potential stressors into opportunities for growth. The benefits extend beyond individual well-being, positively influencing your relationships and interactions with others. By understanding and managing your emotions, you create an environment of empathy and support, fostering a sense of connection and shared understanding.

Life transitions, while challenging, offer a unique opportunity for personal growth and self-discovery. They push us out of our comfort zones, encouraging us to explore new horizons and redefine our identities. With emotional intelligence as your guide, you can navigate these changes with greater ease and confidence. You become adept at recognizing and addressing your emotional needs, fostering resilience and adaptability. As you journey through these transitions, remember that it's okay to feel a mix of emotions. Embrace them as part of the process, using emotional intelligence to guide your responses and actions. By doing so, you transform life's inevitable changes into enriching experiences, paving the way for a future filled with possibility and fulfillment.

10.2 CULTIVATING A CULTURE OF EMOTIONAL INTELLIGENCE

How would you feel if you walked into a place where the air was thick with understanding, respect, and a genuine desire to connect? This is what it means to cultivate a culture of emotional intelligence, where empathy and open communication are not just buzzwords, but the very foundation of how people interact. In such environments, everyone from the CEO to the newest intern shares common values: empathy, respect, and a commitment to understanding one another. Leadership in these spaces isn't a top-down directive but a shared responsibility, with leaders modeling emotional intelligence in their interactions. They listen actively, respond thoughtfully, and encourage the same behavior in their teams. It's about creating a supportive atmosphere where people feel safe to express their emotions and know they'll be met with empathy and understanding.

The benefits of fostering such a culture are as exciting as finding a twenty-dollar bill in your winter coat pocket. Employees feel more engaged and satisfied because they know their voices matter. When people feel heard and understood, their commitment to their work and the organization flourishes. This kind of environment also strengthens community connections. People are more likely to collaborate, support one another, and work towards common goals when they feel valued and respected. The ripple effect of this cultural shift is profound, leading to stronger relationships both within the organization and in the wider community. Collaborative efforts become more successful as individuals bring their best selves to the table, motivated by a shared vision and mutual respect.

So, how do we bring this dreamy culture of emotional intelligence to life? It starts with education and practice. Organizations can implement training programs focused on developing emotional intelligence skills. These programs should cover the basics, self-awareness, empathy, and emotional regulation, and provide practical tools for applying these skills in everyday interactions. Encouraging practices like mindfulness and reflective dialogue can also foster emotional intelligence. Mindfulness helps individuals stay present and engaged, while reflective dialogue encourages open and honest communication. These practices can be introduced through workshops, team-building activities, or even casual lunchtime discussions. The goal is to make emotional intelligence a natural part of the organizational fabric, woven into every conversation and decision.

Consider the story of a school that embraced emotional intelligence as part of its core curriculum. They introduced mindfulness exercises in the classroom and encouraged students to express their emotions openly. The result? Students not only improved their academic performance but also developed stronger social skills and emotional resilience. Teachers reported a decrease in conflicts and an increase in collaboration among students, creating a more harmonious learning environment. This transformation wasn't limited to the students; teachers and staff also embraced emotional intelligence, leading to a more supportive and cohesive school community. The school became a beacon of emotional intelligence, setting an example for others to follow.

In the corporate world, companies that prioritize emotional intelligence often see increased innovation and productivity. Take, for example, a tech company that integrated emotional intelligence training into its leadership development program. By teaching leaders how to communicate empathetically and manage their emotions, the company created a more inclusive and innovative culture. Employees felt empowered to share their ideas and take risks, knowing they would be supported by their peers and leaders. This culture of emotional intelligence led to a surge in creativity and collaboration, resulting in groundbreaking innovations and a stronger competitive edge in the market. Employees reported higher job satisfaction and a greater sense of belonging, reducing turnover and attracting top talent.

Creating a culture of emotional intelligence isn't just a feel-good initiative; it's a strategic advantage. Organizations that prioritize emotional intelligence are better equipped to navigate challenges, adapt to change, and seize new opportunities. They foster an environment where people can thrive, both personally and professionally. As individuals develop their emotional intelligence, they become more resilient, adaptable, and capable of building meaningful relationships. This cultural shift benefits not only the organization but also the broader community, as emotionally intelligent individuals contribute to a more empathetic and understanding world.

As we close this chapter, consider how emotional intelligence can transform your own environment. Whether it's in your workplace, community, or personal life, fostering a culture of empathy and respect can lead to positive, lasting change. It starts with each of us committing to understanding and supporting one another, creating a world where emotional intelligence is the norm, not the exception.

MAKE A DIFFERENCE, AND PLEASE GIVE A REVIEW

UNLOCK THE POWER OF EMOTIONAL INTELLIGENCE

"We make a living by what we get, but we make a life by what we give."

WINSTON CHURCHILL

Your opinion is powerful!

By sharing your thoughts on *'Emotional Intelligence Decoded'*, you're not just reflecting on your own journey, you're giving others the courage and inspiration to begin theirs.

If this book has helped you gain better understanding of your Emotions and given you tips on how to build ongoing beneficial relationships, your story could be the light that someone else needs to make a change. Every review is a ripple that reaches someone who is ready to grow, succeed and thrive.

Why Your Review Matters:

- **Inspire Others:** Your feedback could be the nudge someone needs to invest in themselves and their future.
- **Share Your Wins:** When you highlight what worked for you, you help others see that success is within their reach.
- **Support the Mission:** Your review spreads the message of the benefits of Emotional Intelligence to more people around the world.

How to Write a Review:

1. **Be Honest:** Share your favorite parts, key takeaways, or how the book made a difference in your life.
2. **Keep It Simple:** A few sentences about what you loved is all it takes to make an impact.
3. **Post It Online:** Reviews on Amazon or Goodreads are the best way to help others discover this guide.

We love helping others and hope you will do the same. Thank you!

Freedom Publications

Scan the QR code to leave your review on Amazon

CONCLUSION

What a journey we've been on together! From the moment we first dipped our toes into the vast ocean of emotional intelligence, we've explored its depths, uncovering the treasures that lie beneath. We've laughed, we've pondered, and we've grown, all while learning to navigate the complex currents of our emotions. It's been an adventure, and I'm so grateful to have had you by my side every step of the way.

Throughout this book, we've discovered that emotional intelligence is so much more than just a fancy term. It's a superpower that can transform our lives, our relationships, and even the world around us. We've learned that it's not about being perfect or always knowing the right thing to say. It's about understanding ourselves, empathizing with others, and using that knowledge to make a positive impact.

Remember those five pillars we talked about? Self-awareness, self-regulation, motivation, empathy, and social skills. They're like the building blocks of emotional intelligence, the foundation upon which we can construct a life of meaning and connection. And the best part? They're skills we can all develop, no matter our starting point.

We've explored practical strategies to help us along the way, from self-reflection exercises to emotional regulation techniques. We've discovered the power of active listening, the art of expressing our emotions, and the importance of setting healthy boundaries. These tools are like a trusty compass, guiding us through the sometimes choppy waters of our emotional landscape.

But emotional intelligence isn't just about personal growth; it's about transforming the way we interact with the world. We've seen how it can be applied in the workplace, fostering collaboration and innovation. We've explored how it can strengthen our family bonds, helping us create a home filled with understanding and love. And we've discovered how it can make us better leaders, inspiring others to reach their full potential.

The benefits of embracing emotional intelligence are truly life-changing. Imagine having deeper, more fulfilling relationships, where you can communicate openly and honestly. Picture a work environment where everyone feels valued and supported, leading to increased productivity and job satisfaction. Envision a life where you can face challenges with resilience, bounce back from setbacks, and pursue your dreams with passion and purpose.

But the journey doesn't end here. Developing emotional intelligence is a lifelong process, a continuous unfolding of self-discovery and growth. It's a path that requires courage, vulnerability, and a willingness to step outside our comfort zones. But I promise you, it's a path worth taking.

So, my friend, I invite you to keep learning, keep exploring, and keep growing. Take the insights and strategies you've gained from this book and apply them in your daily life. Start small, be patient with yourself, and celebrate every victory along the way. And remember, you're not alone in this journey. There's a whole community of people out there striving to become the best versions of themselves, just like you.

Together, we can shift the narrative around emotional intelligence from one of misunderstanding to one of empowerment. We can create a world where empathy, respect, and collaboration are the norm, not the exception. A world where we all have the tools to navigate life's challenges with grace and resilience.

So, let's embrace our emotional intelligence with open hearts and curious minds. Let's use it to build bridges, to heal divides, and to create a future that's brighter than we ever thought possible. The journey may not always be easy, but it will always be worth it.

Thank you for joining me on this adventure. Your presence, your insights, and your commitment to growth have been an inspiration. I can't wait to see where your emotional intelligence journey takes you next. Remember, you have the power within you to transform your life and the lives of those around you. All you have to do is take that first step.

With gratitude and encouragement, **Freedom Publications: Your Partner in Personal Growth and Success**

REFERENCES

Salovey, P., & Mayer, J. D. (1990). *Emotional Intelligence. Imagination, Cognition and Personality*, 9(3), 185–211. Sagepub. https://doi.org/10.2190/DUGG-P24E-52WK-6CDG

Goleman, D. (2024). *EI Overview: The Four Domains and Twelve Competencies – Daniel Goleman Emotional Intelligence Courses.* Danielgolemanemotionalintelligence.com. https://danielgolemanemotionalintelligence.com/ei-overview-the-four-domains-and-twelve-competencies/

Clinic, C. (2024, April 6). *What Is the Limbic System?* Cleveland Clinic. https://my.clevelandclinic.org/health/body/limbic-system

Sky Capriolo. (2021, May 13). *The PDQ Guide to EQ Versus IQ; Why EQ is a Better Predictor for Job Success. Motivation Excellence.* https://motivationexcellence.com/2021/05/the-pdq-guide-to-eq-versus-iq-why-eq-is-a-better-predictor-for-job-success/

Understanding Emotional Triggers - Kids First. (2025). Kidsfirstservices.com. https://www.kidsfirstservices.com/first-insights/understanding-emotional-triggers

Journaling for Success: Enhancing Emotional Intelligence. (n.d.). Www.linkedin.com. https://www.linkedin.com/pulse/journaling-success-enhancing-emotional-intelligence-mike

Tang, Y.-Y., Hölzel, B. K., & Posner, M. I. (2015). The neuroscience of mindfulness meditation. *Nature Reviews Neuroscience*, 16(4), 213–225. https://doi.org/10.1038/nrn3916

David, S., & Congleton, C. (2013, November). *Emotional Agility.* Harvard Business Review. https://hbr.org/2013/11/emotional-agility

Stanborough, R. J. (2023, June 5). *How to change negative thinking with cognitive restructuring.* Healthline. https://www.healthline.com/health/cognitive-restructuring

Wikipedia Contributors. (2019, October 27). *Amygdala hijack.* Wikipedia; Wikimedia Foundation. https://en.wikipedia.org/wiki/Amygdala_hijack

Mayo Clinic. (2022, October 11). *Mindfulness exercises.* Mayo Clinic. https://www.mayoclinic.org/healthy-lifestyle/consumer-health/in-depth/mindfulness-exercises/art-20046356

Ozbay, F., Johnson, D. C., Dimoulas, E., Morgan, C., Charney, D., & Southwick, S. (2007). Social Support and Resilience to Stress: From Neurobiology to Clinical Practice. *Psychiatry (Edgmont)*, 4(5), 35. https://pmc.ncbi.nlm.nih.gov/articles/PMC2921311/

REFERENCES

https://www.facebook.com/verywell. (2023, May 19). *Sympathy vs. Empathy: What's the Difference?* Verywell Mind. https://www.verywellmind.com/sympathy-vs-empathy-whats-the-difference-7496474

Wilson, C. (2021, October 29). *How to improve your empathic listening skills: 7 techniques*. Positive Psychology. https://positivepsychology.com/empathic-listening/

Behler, A. M. C., & Berry, D. R. (2022). Closing the empathy gap: A narrative review of the measurement and reduction of parochial empathy. *Social and Personality Psychology Compass, 16*(9). https://doi.org/10.1111/spc3.12701

Selby. (2023, August 21). *Building Empathy Skills: Practical Role Play Scenarios for Learning and Growth | Everyday Speech*. Everyday Speech. https://everydayspeech.com/blog-posts/general/building-empathy-skills-practical-role-play-scenarios-for-learning-and-growth/

What is Emotional Literacy? - Counseling Class [2021] | Study.com. (2021). Study.com. https://study.com/academy/lesson/what-is-emotional-literacy.html

Team, eSoft S. (2023, December 27). *Overcoming Communication Barriers With Emotional Intelligence - Online Business School*. Online Business School - Advance Your Business Skills Online. https://esoftskills.com/overcoming-communication-barriers-with-emotional-intelligence/

The Power of Vulnerability in Dialogue. (2015, March 23). Dialogue Society. https://www.dialoguesociety.org/column/the-power-of-vulnerability-in-dialogue/

Woffindin, L. (2024, September 6). *The Role of Emotional Intelligence in Conflict Resolution*. CPD Online College. https://cpdonline.co.uk/knowledge-base/mental-health/emotional-intelligence-conflict-resolution/

Reid, S. (2022, July 6). *Setting Healthy Boundaries in Relationships*. HelpGuide.org. https://www.helpguide.org/relationships/social-connection/setting-healthy-boundaries-in-relationships

What is Empathy and how can it benefit my relationships. (n.d.). Master's Counselling Calgary. https://www.masterscounselling.com/what-is-empathy-and-how-can-it-benefit-my-relationships

Molinsky, A., & Hahn, M. (2024, February 29). *Building Cross-Cultural Relationships in a Global Workplace*. Harvard Business Review. https://hbr.org/2024/02/building-cross-cultural-relationships-in-a-global-workplace

Raising Emotionally Intelligent Children - HelpGuide.org. (2019, August 13). HelpGuide.org. https://www.helpguide.org/family/parenting/raising-emotionally-intelligent-children

Lofgren, J. (2024, November 12). *Empathetic Leadership: The Key to Building Trust and High-Performing Teams | FranklinCovey*. FranklinCovey. https://www.franklincovey.com/blog/empathetic-leadership/

5 Steps to Building an Emotionally Intelligent Team. (n.d.). HSI. https://hsi.com/blog/5-steps-to-building-an-emotionally-intelligent-team

Woffindin, L. (2024, September 6). *The Role of Emotional Intelligence in Conflict Resolution.* CPD Online College. https://cpdonline.co.uk/knowledge-base/mental-health/emotional-intelligence-conflict-resolution/

Issah, M. (2018). Change leadership: the Role of Emotional Intelligence. *SAGE Open, 8*(3), 1–6. sagepub. https://doi.org/10.1177/2158244018800910

Cleven, A. J., Renaud, A., Larose-Pierre, M., McQuade, B., Griffin, B. L., Johnson, C., & Hughes, J. A. (2023). Associating Growth Mindset with Emotional Intelligence and Why It's Needed for Professional Identity Formation. *American Journal of Pharmaceutical Education, 87*(6), 100110. https://doi.org/10.1016/j.ajpe.2023.100110

How to Overcome Your Inner Critic. (n.d.). Choosing Therapy. https://www.choosingtherapy.com/overcome-inner-critic/

Moeller, R. W., Seehuus, M., & Peisch, V. (2020). Emotional Intelligence, Belongingness, and Mental Health in College Students. *Frontiers in Psychology, 11*(93). https://doi.org/10.3389/fpsyg.2020.00093

Connor-Savarda, B.-N. (2022, June 1). *Emotionally Intelligent Leaders Across History and How to Emulate Them.* EI Magazine. https://www.ei-magazine.com/post/emotionally-intelligent-leaders-across-history-and-how-to-emulate-them

LID Publishing. (2023, November 6). *Debunking The Myths About Emotional Intelligence with Nicole Soames - LID Publishing.* LID Publishing. https://lidpublishing.com/2023/11/06/debunking-the-myths-about-emotional-intelligence-with-nicole-soames/

hapman, S., & Rupured, M. (2024, February 19). *Time Management: 10 Strategies for Better Time Management.* Extension.uga.edu. https://extension.uga.edu/publications/detail.html?number=C1042&title=time-management-10-strategies-for-better-time-management

McGarvie, S. (2024, September 10). *Developing Emotional Maturity: 11 Methods & Worksheets.* PositivePsychology.com. https://positivepsychology.com/emotional-maturity/

How to Develop Emotional Intelligence in Your Learning Programs. (n.d.). EI Design. https://www.eidesign.net/how-to-develop-emotional-intelligence-in-your-learning-programs/

Thompkins, S. (2023, August 28). *Emotional intelligence and leadership effectiveness.* Center for Creative Leadership. https://www.ccl.org/articles/leading-effectively-articles/emotional-intelligence-and-leadership-effectiveness/

ManageMagazine, T. (2023, November 16). *The 10 Benefits of Emotional Intelligence in the Workplace*. ManageMagazine. https://managemagazine.com/article-bank/emotions-emotional-intelligence/the-10-benefits-of-emotional-intelligence-in-the-workplace/

How to Navigate Life Transitions with Emotional Resilience. (2025). Herserenity.com. https://www.herserenity.com/blog/how-to-navigate-life-transitions-with-emotional-resilience

Emotionally, an. (2021, June 29). *CultureAlly*. CultureAlly . https://www.cultureally.com/blog/creatinganemotionallyintelligentworkplace

ABOUT THE PUBLISHER

Freedom Publications is a respected name in business literature and Self Help books, dedicated to providing readers from all walks of life with the tools and insights to succeed in today's competitive and ever-evolving world. Our books cater to teams, leaders, managers, entrepreneurs, professionals, executives, and everyday individuals; young and old, eager to sharpen their skills, elevate their thinking, and make impactful changes in their careers and lives.

Our books are carefully crafted to deliver practical, accessible guidance on everything from building cohesive teams and inspiring effective leadership to boosting productivity and achieving personal and professional goals. With a focus on real-world applications, our books empower readers to turn concepts into actionable strategies that benefit both individuals and groups, enabling stronger communication, smarter decision-making, and sustained success across any field.

Whether you're a business leader striving to lead your team with vision, a professional looking to grow your skill set, an entrepreneur ready to take your venture to the next level, or simply someone interested in improving everyday effectiveness, Freedom Publications is your essential resource for the insights and knowledge to thrive in every aspect of modern business.

Freedom Publications: Your Partner in Personal Growth and Success.